DATE DUE

MY01 '09			

DEMCO 38-297

ESSENTIALS OF MEDIA PLANNING

A MARKETING VIEWPOINT

SECOND EDITION

ARNOLD M. BARBAN

The University of Texas at Austin

STEVEN M. CRISTOL

U.S. Marketing Services

FRANK J. KOPEC

Rumrill-Hoyt, Inc.

 NTC Business Books
a division of National Textbook Company • Lincolnwood Illinois U.S.A.

Table of Contents

Foreword

Herbert M. Baum
President, Campbell U.S.A.
Campbell Soup Company
Chairman, Association of National Advertisers

A marketing perspective on the media planning process is critical to optimizing the effectiveness of a total marketing plan. That's why this book is so important in helping the reader to understand that media planning is more than CPM's and reach/frequency and all the other statistical measurements that seem to take the place of creativity and judgement in media planning.

As you work your way through this book, you'll learn how marketing plans influence the way media are evaluated—and how the various elements of the marketing mix interact with media planning.

I urge you to pay close attention. Don't fall into the trap so often attributed to mediocrity in media, that is, the viewing of media planning as the task of *efficiently* distributing or allocating advertising dollars. Almost an accounting function.

I urge you to look at media planning as an important step in the creative process. Read the material to learn the various strategies and tactics possible to turn statistical analysis and knowledge of the marketplace into creative media thinking.

Media and marketing are going through an evolution from a national, to a regional or local perspective. *Essentials of Media Planning* will involve you in weighting by target market and geographic region. You'll learn the importance of demographics, psychographics and product usage variables—all the things beyond broad statistical comparison that will help you make creative media decisions in tune with the changing marketplace.

Work with this book. Read it. Reread it. Make the most of the synergies between traditional media planning and the new input of marketing planning to arrive at a creative media plan.

Preface

In the Preface to the first edition of this book, we said the following:

> Too often, and among too many advertisers and agencies, the
> Media Department is looked upon as a support function instead
> of as a vital problem-solving arm of marketing and advertising
> management. Media planning has frequently been a hero in delivering
> marketing results, but seldom gets the credit it deserves. The "big
> idea" that makes an advertising campaign successful doesn't always
> have to come from a copywriter's (or art director's) desk. Why not
> from the desk of a media planner? The only limitation on the
> potential for media decisions to spark any marketing program is the
> tendency to underestimate the importance of good media planning.

Is the situation today different from that which sparked our first edition comments? The answer seemingly is yes and no. Take what one media expert, Ed Papazian, recently said about the evolution of the media department:

> There's been a good deal of publicity in the past few years about
> the rising status of the media function at the ad agencies, and not
> without justification. Whereas a decade ago the drive was on to
> reduce such departments, trim ancillary expenses, use computers to
> do media work "more efficiently," etc., things are quite different
> now. Media department staffs are increasing, the pay is better, and
> management is more supportive and appreciative of media's role in
> deciphering the new technologies, exploring alternative media forms
> such as cable, barter syndication, etc. Indeed, in a recent realignment,
> a major agency upped its media director into its top management
> ranks, while the head of a Midwestern shop went out of his way to
> praise the media role at his agency.

The surveys seem to bear this out. In most cases, while copy ranks
as the most important agency function, media is a close second
(according to clients), vying with the account execs for favor.[1]

Others, although perhaps agreeing that the status of the media function has been elevated in recent years, would argue that media decisions
still are not accorded their rightful importance and that media people
should be more forceful in advocating their contribution. For example,
Craig Reiss, New York bureau chief of *Advertising Age* and national
media editor, stated:

This argument (whether media or creative is more important) is
more than just a question of who deserves credit for success. The
agency people in media departments suffer from a weak self-image.
They tell themselves the most important function of an ad agency is to
produce spectacularly effective creative. They concede creative always
will be more important than media.
On that count, I disagree—a lot. . . .
Media strategy is the most an agency has to offer in terms of the
entire marketing approach. And use of media, more than creative,
sells product. In that case, it seems strange to me that we don't see
more media executives heading up agencies. If the media mavens ever
stop being humble about their craft, maybe that will change.[2]

Regardless of the status actually accorded media decisions and media
people, one of the aims of this book is to offer its readers a solid foundation for media selection decisions by focusing on the higher decision-
making levels of objectives and strategy that must precede the tactical
considerations of media selection. By treating this subject in a marketing framework, we recognize that media activity is an integral part of
the marketing mix and should be examined in the context of its
interrelationships with other marketing variables.

This is not, then, another book on media selection. Several knowl-
edgeable authors have written instructive works on the tactical aspects
of evaluating alternatives in selecting advertising media; however, because of the pressures to move ahead and choose the communication
vehicles that will carry the advertising to consumers, too little energy
has been devoted to the study of media objectives and strategy. Accordingly, this book is written to encourage readers to develop a marketing-
oriented approach to selecting media through a better understanding of
the fundamentals of media planning. The authors do not intend to provide rules or hard-and-fast answers, but hope to stimulate readers to

raise important questions in conceiving a media plan and to use imagination in creating solutions to media problems.

More specifically, how should this book be used and how is it tailored to the individual reader's needs? Among advertising practitioners, the experienced decision maker will find a concise, back-to-basics overview of media planning fundamentals. To provide the neophyte with an orientation to media planning, agencies and advertisers can use the book in both formal and informal training programs. Regardless of career stage, anyone with a position in brand management, agency account management, or media planning will find that the principles explained in these pages can be applied to help media achieve advertising and marketing goals.

In colleges and universities, this book will help advertising students conceptualize a media plan and judge its place in the marketing mix. Educators will find that this book not only provides basic input for media courses, but fits in well as supplementary material for general advertising and marketing courses. In principles courses as well as in integrative courses in the management, planning and campaigns aspects of marketing, promotion, and advertising, we hope to provide students with additional insight into the media aspects of the advertising function.

We want to emphasize to the readers of this book—practitioners and students alike—that we are not attempting to provide a complete textbook on the topic of media planning, but rather a primer. As stated earlier, *Essentials of Media Planning* is a back-to-basics overview of media planning fundamentals, and we encourage readers to supplement the reading here with that of a currently available textbook.

We are especially pleased to include in the appendix of this edition several actual media plans developed for well-known national advertisers by highly respected agencies. It is hoped that these plans provide good insight into the media planning process. We gratefully acknowledge the substantial contribution of the companies and individuals who provided these plans. The authors also wish to express a deep appreciation to all the companies that permitted us the use of copyrighted materials and for their assistance in securing the needed information for tables and figures. Special thanks are extended to Mediamark Research Inc., Simmons Market Research Bureau, and Telmar Group Inc.

Arnold M. Barban
Steven M. Cristol
Frank J. Kopec

Endnotes

1. Ed Papazian, "The Evolution of the Media Department," *Marketing and Media Decisions,* October 1985, p. 90.

2. Craig Reiss, "Creativity Bows to Media Use," *Advertising Age,* March 10, 1986, p. 24.

Chapter One

A Brief Introduction to Media Planning

What do you do for a product that enjoys such widespread consumer awareness that its label has been a vanguard of the pop art explosion? Consumer acceptance is no problem; if you open the kitchen cabinet of the average American home, you'll find about seven cans of the product on the shelf. The product's marketing mix is a well-oiled machine with no obvious flaws. So what do you do to improve the marketing effort?

Media pro Herb Maneloveg relates that this was a problem he faced while media director at the BBDO advertising agency. The product: Campbell's Soup. The marketing solution: changes in the media plan. Reconsideration of media objectives and strategies produced a revised media schedule that put Campbell's Soup advertising on pre-lunchtime radio. The result: radio contributed to a substantial sales volume increase attributed to more frequent use of soup for lunch.

What Is Media Planning?

In an early book on the subject of advertising media, practitioner and journalist Roger Barton wrote of the need to relate media planning and marketing planning.[1] This approach represented a change from earlier days when media decisions typically consisted of clerical functions dealing mostly with the buying of advertising media.

Accordingly, media planning today can be viewed as *the process of designing a course of action that shows how advertising time and space will be used to contribute to the achievement of marketing objectives.*

1

The Terminology of Planning

As a key stepping-stone to developing an understanding of media planning, it is important to distinguish between the three most misunderstood words in the managerial planning vocabulary: *objective, strategy,* and *tactics.*

An *objective* is simply a statement of the task one wishes to accomplish. A *strategy* is the means prescribed for attaining the objective, and *tactics* are the specific, detailed activities required for implementation of the strategy. Implicit in these definitions is the fact that objectives are the highest order of planning, strategies are the next highest, and tactics are the lowest. Accordingly, strategies should derive from objectives, and tactics should in turn derive from strategies.

Consider a simple example. Let's say you have a month of vacation time and want to go to Europe. Getting to Europe is your *objective.* Then you must decide whether to travel by air or by sea. Whatever mode of transportation you choose becomes your *strategy* for accomplishing the objective of getting to Europe. If you choose air travel, you must then concern yourself with such *tactics* as making airline reservations for a specific time to facilitate the implementation of your strategy.

Just as your strategy decision involved the evaluation of alternative modes of travel, your tactical decisions involve the evaluation of multiple alternatives. Which airline should you choose? Should you fly first class or economy? What time of day will you depart? While there will be some constraints on the number of options available to you, each question gives you several alternatives from which to choose. It is precisely this type of situation that characterizes most media decisions.

Objectives, strategy, and tactics, as well as the relationships between them, will be discussed in the media planning context in subsequent chapters. If you desire further explanation as to the differences or relationships between these terms, we suggest you consult any management principles textbook.[2]

Inputs to the Media Plan

The media planning function does not operate in a vacuum. The media plan is but one of many components in the overall marketing plan, and interacts as such with other elements of that total plan. These elements include product characteristics, distribution channels, promotion mix, packaging, and pricing policy. Overall marketing objectives, as well as objectives within each of these areas, serve as vital inputs to the media plan. Many uncontrollable factors, such as the competitive situation and economic conditions, also have important implications for media decisions at the planning level.

(Chapter 2 is devoted to a more detailed explanation of how both the marketing plan and uncontrollable factors affect media planning.)

Components of the Media Plan

There are five basic components of the media plan: (1) background review, (2) statement of objectives, (3) target market definition, (4) media mix, and (5) overall scheduling considerations.

A good way to begin the media plan is with a background review that puts everyone involved with the plan on common ground in their assumptions and knowledge of the brand. The plan should then review marketing and advertising objectives and state the media objectives the plan is designed to accomplish. The target market must be precisely defined so that the most appropriate *media vehicles* can be selected. Media vehicle usually refers to a specific publication or program such as *Reader's Digest* or ''CBS Evening News''; *media type* refers to a class of media, such as magazines or television. Which media types will be used and what relative levels of effectiveness are expected from each are questions that the plan must answer by outlining the mix of media. Finally, the media plan must include an explanation of how media are scheduled within a given time parameter.

These five components taken together do not produce a complete media plan; rather, they serve as the foundation of the plan. (They will be examined in detail in Chapters 3, 4 and 5.) The media plan will, of course, include both statistical and qualitative rationales for the specific media approaches recommended. From this point forward, however, our concern for these tactical considerations will be minor, as our attention will focus on media decisions at higher levels.

The Need for Flexibility In Media Planning

Marketing objectives are a fundamental input to media planning and it is important to understand both the limitations of these objectives and the effects these limitations have on media planning. An integral part of the formulation of marketing objectives is sales forecasting which—like any type of forecasting—is done with some degree of uncertainty. Even with the highly sophisticated statistical techniques employed in forecasting, it is not uncommon to witness substantial variations between real sales and expectations, frequently because of actions by competitors.

Unexpected sales results, whether favorable or unfavorable, may require significant adjustments in the media plan, even during its execution. Other factors, such as competitive reactions or the failure or success of the creative approach in one of the media vehicles, will also call for adjustment in the plan. Thus, we can see the need for flexibility in media planning to allow for rapid shifting of gears when new circumstances indicate a need for plan modification.

To fulfill this need, some media planners prepare alternate, or *standby,* plans. Each standby media plan corresponds to an expected different development in sales results expressed in varying degrees of potential sales increases or declines. Other planners say that it is often better to incorporate *options* into the basic plan than to develop completely different plans based on contingencies. Both of these viewpoints recognize the importance of flexibility in media planning.

An Overview of the Media Decision-Making Process

Figure 1.1 explains graphically some of the things discussed thus far in this chapter—as well as elements to be dealt with in subsequent chapters. The purpose of the chart is to show, in a relatively simple format, the totality of the media decision making process. The boxed elements —background inputs, objectives, strategies, etc.—indicate some of the major factors or variables considered in the development of a media plan. The items in an ellipse—integration, planning, implementation, evaluation—designate the functional relationships that link various decision areas. There are not many definitive decision rules in existence today that establish the necessary functional relationships for efficient media decision making. There will, though, be research in the future that adds to the knowledge base.

Some additional highlights of the overview are:

• Most media planners typically start the process with background inputs and continue in sequence, following the direction of the arrows. However, constraints and uncontrollable influences must be taken into account throughout the process—and a decision maker would not wait until tactics are in place before considering them (the box is shown in dashed lines to indicate this circumstance).

- Objectives are hierarchical—marketing goals are established first, followed by advertising, and finally, the media objectives are set.

- The five types of strategies shown are exemplary rather than exhaustive. Based on the specific product, service, or idea advertised, there may be other strategies to establish.

- Tactical executions involve decision making, but generally of a lesser order than strategies. The same type of hierarchy is present among the types of tactics specified; for example, decisions regarding vehicle selection will usually be of more consequence than the bookkeeping system used to pay bills and receive commission income.

- Once a media effort has been determined from background inputs and constraints—and objectives, strategies, and tactics are carefully enunciated—the plan is put into action (that is, ads and commercials appear in various media vehicles). This will produce an audience/market impact; and that impact could be positive, negative, or neutral depending upon the plan's objectives and the nature of the marketplace. The measurement of the impact involves an attempt to assess the relative contribution of the media program to overall advertising effectiveness—which, from our current understanding of how advertising works, is a most difficult task!

- Once the plan is executed and the market impact has been measured (either formally through research testing or informal experiences), a postmortem evaluation should be conducted. The decision maker can then decide what adjustments in thinking are necessary to improve the next plan. The evaluation analyses thus provide feedback on the total process and serve as background input for the next stage of the plan. Thus, each successive stage of media decision making should benefit from its predecessor and result in the establishment of dynamic relationships over time.

Figure 1.1

Overview of the Media Decision-Making Process

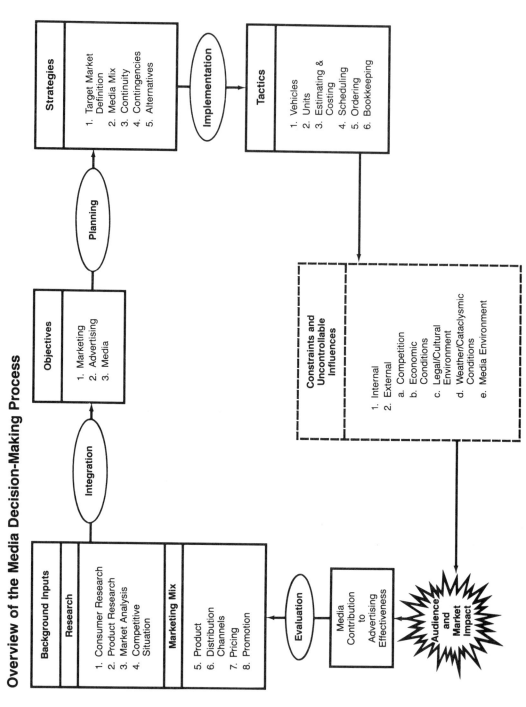

Summary

The brevity of this introductory chapter makes it unnecessary to present a topical summary and review. But it is crucial that you emerge from this reading with the understanding that media planning, as a subsystem of marketing planning, is concerned with how to use advertising time and space most effectively to contribute to the achievement of marketing objectives. These objectives, along with the various elements of the marketing mix and certain uncontrollable factors, interact with media decision-making and exert profound influence on the media plan. Chapter 2 will examine the nature of this influence.

Endnotes

1. Roger Barton, *Media in Advertising* (New York: McGraw-Hill Book Co., 1964), pp. 19-22.
2. See, for example: John D. Leckenby and Nugent Wedding, *Advertising Management* (Columbus, Ohio: Grid Publishing, Inc., 1982).

Chapter Two

How Marketing Planning Affects Media Planning

Media problems are marketing problems. Your ability to make media decisions will continue to grow as you develop an understanding of the marketing and advertising influences on media planning.

How Marketing Plans Influence Media Plans

The marketing plan begins with the product itself and outlines the distribution, pricing, and promotion requirements for that product. It is usually prepared on an annual basis and carries with it a budget for executing the entire marketing program for the year. Since the media budget will be a portion of this marketing budget, the marketing plan determines the amount of financial resources available to the media planner.

This financial influence is just one of many aspects of the marketing plan's effect on media planning. We will now examine the influence of product characteristics, distribution channels, pricing policy, and the promotion mix.

Product Characteristics

Every level of media planning—objectives, strategy, and tactics—may be affected by product characteristics. Media objectives are likely to be influenced by the product's present stage in the product life cycle (see Figure 2.1).[1] Because creating awareness is so important for new products, media objectives for these products often emphasize the necessity of reaching the largest possible percentage of the target market within the shortest acceptable period of time. For an established product in the maturity stage of the life cycle, reminder advertising might call for media objectives that maximize the number of impressions delivered. Chapter 4 will present a more detailed discussion of using the product life cycle as an input to the formulation of media objectives.

Figure 2.1

Typical Product Life Cycle

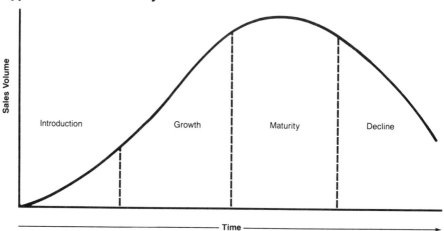

The product life cycle has traditionally been thought of as four stages:
(1) introduction, (2) growth, (3) maturity, and (4) decline. At the introductory stage, product awareness is low and only a small percentage of the total potential market is using the product. Products in the growth stage enjoy more widespread adoption and an upward trend in demand, but they have not yet reached their full market potential. Demand for the established product will mature when the market is saturated, and eventually demand diminishes and the product dies.

At the strategy level, product characteristics may affect media *weighting*—that is, what balance of media types will be used to achieve media objectives. The actual physical characteristics of the product are particularly significant as a weighting consideration. Food products, for example, frequently are heavily advertised in magazines because that medium's high quality of mechanical reproduction offers excellent opportunity for appealing to the appetite through a mouth-watering visual presentation of the product. On the other hand, food products that are purchased every few days may require a medium such as television that can communicate with the consumer in a time span that is more attuned to the product's repurchase cycle.

At the tactical level of media decisions, physical characteristics of the product may affect media vehicle selection. Suppose you are introducing a new model automobile and you have already included magazines in your media strategy. If you want the consumer to get a close-up look at the long, streamlined body of the automobile, the $8\frac{3}{16}$" $\times$ $10\frac{7}{8}$" pages in *Time* will be better suited to your communication needs than the smaller $5\frac{1}{8}$" $\times$ $7\frac{3}{8}$" pages in *TV Guide*.

The influence of product features on media can be seen in the example of Polaroid camera advertising. When Polaroid introduced a camera that developed its own color photos in 60 seconds, a series of 60-second television spots were required when it was decided to actually demonstrate the product in use.

Distribution Channels

Geographic Patterns. Distribution activities are concerned with making the product readily available to consumers by moving the product to the right place at the right time. More often than not, the "right place" does not include all geographic areas within the country. Many brands of beer in the United States, for example, are distributed on a strictly regional basis. And some products, such as high fashion items like designer dresses from a well-known couturier, may be distributed from coast to coast—but only in major metropolitan areas. Thus we see the first limitation that distribution places on the media plan. Wasted coverage is the simple result of delivering advertising messages to consumers in places where the product is not available and will not be available in the near future.

Media experts Jack Sissors and Jim Surmanek add additional light to the matter of coordinating distribution and media planning.

There are a number of answers to the question of where to advertise. The simplest, of course, is to advertise wherever the brand is distributed. Obviously, it is usually a waste of money to advertise in a geographical market where the brand is not distributed. Occasionally, however, the objective may be to force distribution by creating a demand for a brand through advertising, even though the brand is not distributed in the market. When the planner has this objective, it makes sense to advertise before distribution is available.

Beyond the obvious answer, however, is the question of whether it is better to advertise in geographical markets where sales for a given brand have been good, or where sales have not been good.[2]

Distributors' Reactions to Different Media. Distribution may affect the media plan in another way if members of the distribution channel voice their opinions about certain types of media. Some dealers may favor local media with which they are more intimately acquainted, while others favor types of media that they feel lend prestige to the product, such as network television. It is sometimes necessary to make adjustments in media weighting or specific vehicle selection based on these considerations, if the advertiser is to maintain good relations with his channel members. In fact, channel members in some cases become so important that they are listed as a target audience for the media plan.

Equalizing Regional Sales Force Impact. Relations between the sales force and channel members can also affect media planning. Suppose that a product is distributed nationally but the amount of contact between the sales force and dealers varies from one region to the next. If the sales force on the West coast, for example, is able to make significantly more calls than the sales force in the Midwest, there is a weakness in midwestern distribution because of fewer contacts with dealers. The media plan can help equalize total contacts by increasing the allocation for trade advertising in regions where contacts are weakest.

Market Exposure and Distribution Policies. The degree of market exposure that distribution channels afford the product also influences media decisions. Distribution for a product may be *intensive, selective* or *exclusive.*[3] Intensive distribution makes the product available to virtually any wholesaler or retailer who wishes to sell it, and it follows that this type of distribution provides the highest degree of overall market exposure. An example of an intensively distributed product is women's hosiery, which is distributed at retail through supermarkets, drug stores, department stores, discount stores, women's clothing shops, and even convenience stores.

Selective distribution is the policy of selecting those dealers who are best able to serve the manufacturer. Many high quality brands of men's shirts are selectively distributed to men's stores and the better department stores.

Exclusive distribution is generally based on a formal agreement between the manufacturer and a small number of distributors in each market. An example is automobile distribution, in which there may be only one outlet for each line of automobiles in smaller communities.

How do these different distribution policies affect media planning? This can best be answered in terms of the amount of merchandising support that manufacturers can expect from dealers. With exclusive distribution, dealers generally provide substantial advertising and sales promotion support at the local level. It is much more difficult, however, to get dealer support when the product is intensively distributed. In that situation the manufacturer must rely more heavily on his or her media coverage to bear the burden of promotion. We can therefore see that media planning may again play an equalizing role where market exposure is heavy but dealer support is difficult to obtain.

Personality of Retail Outlets. Each retail store has a personality, or image, as perceived by the consumer. The store's interior design, the price and quality of merchandise it carries, and the tone of its advertisements all contribute to store personality.

Various media vehicles have personalities, too. The types of retail outlets in the product's distribution channel influence the media plan to the extent that the store personality and the personality of media to be used should be as consistent as possible. For example, a diamond importer that distributes its diamonds through retailers such as Tiffany's, which has an extremely sophisticated store personality, is more likely to advertise in *New Yorker* than in *Reader's Digest*.

Pricing Policy and Strategy

Before examining the effects of pricing on the media plan, it is important to point out that it is somewhat less than entirely accurate to discuss pricing in the context of controllable marketing variables. In many industries, pricing is largely determined by competitive forces and in some others it is influenced by the government.

With these constraints in mind, we can isolate three ways in which pricing policy influences the media plan. First, pricing directly affects profit margins, which in turn affect the amount of money available for advertising. It follows that this effect on the advertising budget will influence the quality and quantity of media buys.

Secondly, margins within the distribution channel may affect the amount of dealer support that the advertiser can expect from channel members. When the wholesaler's or retailer's margin is small, there is less incentive to give promotional support to the manufacturer. Large margins for these channel members, however, tend to elicit a greater degree of support. The effect on the media plan is that if pricing policy results in larger margins for dealers (relative to margins offered by competitors), the ensuing promotional support originating at the wholesale/retail level may reduce the manufacturer's need for media expenditures. Wholesaler support, by helping to promote a product to the retail trade, may reduce the amount of money allocated to trade media for advertising to retailers. Likewise, retailer support that helps promote a product to consumers may reduce the manufacturer's investment in consumer advertising in each local market.

The third pricing influence on the media plan is the result of the interaction between pricing strategy and product characteristics. Because price is often perceived by the consumer as an indicator of quality, many high-quality products carry prestige prices. A prestigious product image cannot be fully expressed in creative execution alone; the creative appeal must be delivered in a medium that helps to convey the quality and prestigious image that price and product characteristics merit.

Promotion

Because the media plan is a component of the promotion mix, every activity within this mix has some significant effect on the media planning function.

How Promotion Plans Affect Media Plans

Advertising, sales promotion, and personal selling combine in varying degrees to form a unique promotion mix for every product or service. Whenever "product" is mentioned, we almost always mean this to include service and idea advertising as well. Each of these promotion subsystems has crucial effects on media planning, but perhaps the most pervasive media implications lie in the general promotion strategy employed.

General Promotion Strategy

The tremendous interaction between promotion and distribution is such that promotion is the primary tool with which a producer of goods can secure cooperation from channel members. The two basic promotion methods are the *push strategy* and the *pull strategy*. These strategies are executed through very different combinations of advertising, sales promotion, and personal selling. Different combinations of promotion mix components may, of course, suggest different media plans.

When a push strategy is employed, promotion efforts are aimed primarily at channel members so that the producer can push its product through the channel to the consumer. A push strategy usually relies heavily on trade advertising, personal selling transactions with channel members and dealer promotions, such as special incentive plans.

Producers using a pull strategy attempt to build brand demand through consumer advertising (and consumer promotions, such as coupons, sweepstakes, and contests) which is the focus of their promotion mix. Stimulated demand is manifest when consumers ask prospective channel members for the brand; thus, consumers pull the product through the distribution channel when the advertising has been effective in bringing about the desired behavioral change.

The potential for using each type of promotion strategy depends heavily on the marketer's position as perceived by consumers and the trade. For example, we could expect Procter & Gamble to introduce a new detergent successfully by using a pull strategy because of the company's reputation and established performance in the detergent industry. It is unlikely, however, that the same strategy would work for a detergent introduced by a marketer who has no experience or reputation in the household cleaner category.

The type of general promotion strategy employed is reflected throughout the media plan. Allocation of a $20,000,000 promotion budget for two producers of household detergents—one using a push strategy and the other using a pull strategy—might look like this:

	Co.A (Push)	Co.B (Pull)
Consumer Media Advertising	$1,200,000	$13,700,000
Trade Media Advertising	1,600,000	200,000
Personal Selling	9,000,000	4,000,000
Consumer Sales Promotion	200,000	2,000,000
Dealer Sales Promotion	8,000,000	100,000
Total	$20,000,000	$20,000,000

In relation to this hypothetical example, it is important to note that $1,600,000 invested in trade advertising buys much more advertising space than a similar amount of money invested in consumer advertising, since media rates are significantly higher in consumer media than in trade media. And yet, while consumer rates are higher in terms of absolute costs, they tend to be lower than trade rates in terms of cost per prospect reached.

At the tactical level of the media plan, we might expect to see the following vehicles selected within the magazine medium:

Company A (Push)	Company B (Pull)
Progressive Grocer	*Family Circle*
Supermarket Business	*Woman's Day*
Grocery Marketing	*Good Housekeeping*
Supermarket News	*Ladies' Home Journal*

Also consider, however, that consumer advertising may be used as an indirect means of trade advertising. Referring to what was said earlier in this chapter about distributors' reactions to different media, it is interesting to note that a marketer might use highly visible consumer media, such as the "Tonight Show" and "Monday Night Football," solely for its effect on the trade.

Now that you are acquainted with the fundamental ways in which the two types of promotion strategy affect media, we can examine the specific effects of advertising, personal selling, and sales promotion on media planning.

Advertising

Three aspects of the advertising plan especially influence media decisions: (1) advertising objectives, (2) positioning and (3) message content.

Advertising Objectives: The Nature of Communication Goals. Since 1961, when the Association of National Advertisers published Russell Colley's important book, *Defining Advertising Goals for Measured Advertising Results* (DAG-MAR), it has been generally acknowledged that advertising objectives should be stated as communication goals. Advertising alone, except in some direct response situations, does not do the complete marketing job; its function is to communicate. By having communication tasks quantifiably defined in terms of audience, degree, and time period, we will not only be able to measure advertising results more accurately—which is Colley's concern—but will also be able to do a better job of establishing specific media objectives and formulating media strategies.

To understand the relationship between communication goals and media decisions, it is helpful to conceptualize a marketing communication spectrum as shown in Figure 2.2.

Figure 2.2

The Marketing Communication Spectrum

When a consumer is exposed to an effective advertising message over time, he or she first becomes aware of it *(awareness)* and eventually understands it *(knowledge);* once the message is favorably accepted *(acceptance),* he or she may decide that the next time this type of product is bought, the advertised brand likely will be chosen *(conviction).* If the consumer has already used the brand, the conviction goal may be stated in terms of achieving or maintaining brand loyalty. Finally, the consumer makes the actual purchase *(action).* It is reasonable to state advertising goals in terms of moving X percent of the target market, within a period of X time units to any stage on this spectrum, as far up as the conviction stage. (Because advertising alone usually cannot be directly correlated with sales, it must have the help of the rest of the marketing mix to ensure that the consumer moves the final step to the action stage.)

How do advertising objectives stated in terms of various stages on this spectrum affect the media plan? If the advertising goal is stated in terms of achieving awareness, for example, the media plan will usually be concerned with delivering the message to the largest possible percentage of the target market in a certain time period. Because we are often communicating a new idea when trying to achieve awareness, the major portion of the media budget might be allocated to television, which can use intrusive sight and sound to demonstrate the unfamiliar. Thus, by compelling the delivery of the message to a large percentage of the target market, and by influencing media weighting, the advertising communication goal of increasing awareness has directly affected media planning at the objective level and strategy level, respectively.

Some advertising experts advocate an even more direct relationship between communication goals and media planning. They suggest that communication goals should be interpreted in such a way that subsidiary communication goals can be derived from them. These subsidiary goals should be narrow enough to be assigned an individual medium or combination of media. If objectives are too broad to handle in this manner, they must be refined and divided into component parts.

Chapter 4 will offer a foundation to make you better equipped to study the effects of communications goals on media objectives. More examples of these effects will be explained in greater detail in that chapter.

Positioning. Thus far in this chapter, we have seen some of the ways that elements of the marketing mix affect media planning. In some measure, positioning—that is, strategy that will create a "position" for a product in the "prospect's mind"[4]—may influence all areas of the marketing mix and therefore indirectly affect media decisions. In other words, we can conceptualize positioning's effects on media planning as a two-step process. In the first step, positioning strategy affects other marketing activities. In the second step, marketing activities—as modified by positioning—influence media planning in the many ways discussed in this chapter. So the effects of positioning on media planning are largely indirect and not necessarily clear-cut.

Another positioning consideration is competitive media usage. For a product that is not the leader in its market, positioning theory suggests that this product should avoid trying to beat the leader head-on. The media implication is that it may not be desirable to advertise this product in the same media used by the market leader, since the underdog advertiser would run the risk of consumers attributing sponsorship of the message to the market leader. However, if a product is not the market leader—yet has a demonstrable advantage—one option is indeed to meet the competition head-on.

Message Content. The nature of the message and its specific contents affect media planning at every level. At the objectives level, for example, employing the creative technique of reminder advertising will require emphasis in media objectives on the frequency of impressions delivered.

At the strategy level, selection of media type is influenced by the nature of the message. A message announcing something newsworthy, such as a product innovation, may be more effectively delivered in the informational environment of the newspaper medium. Messages revolving around demonstration of the product are particularly well suited to television. And, as noted previously, the excellent quality of reproduction available in magazines enhances the opportunity for food-producing companies to appeal to the consumer's appetite through visual display.

At the tactical level, the media planner must consider message content in fulfilling the responsibility of providing the most appropriate vehicle for the message. In print media, certain vehicles may exclusively offer a space unit that fits the message's layout especially well. *Better Homes and Gardens,* for example, offers more than 101 different space units for sale. A content analysis of media vehicles is also useful in discovering media selection opportunities. This is illustrated in the case of New England Life Insurance Company which, for several years, used a cartoon format for its advertising messages. New England Life found *New Yorker* magazine to be an excellent vehicle for delivering those cartoon messages, since *New Yorker* has gained notoriety for the sophisticated cartoons that are found throughout every issue. Readership of ads should be enhanced as a result of how well they blend with the editorial content of the media vehicle.

A word of caution about considering creative requirements in selecting media: choosing a media type or vehicle that is best suited to the message's creative requirements does not always result in spending media dollars in the most efficient way.

Consider the following case from an era in which television commercials typically were not in color. Media expert Richard P. Jones explains:

A well-known advertiser in the household products field introduced a new colored brand (Brand A). The creative group devised an excellent campaign using four-color, full-page magazine advertisements. The objective of this approach was to dramatize the new colors and give the product a high quality, decorator image. Copy tests revealed an excellent reaction and good playback of copy points. . . .

The strategy might well have worked except for one factor. A leading competitor came out with a similar product (Brand B) shortly thereafter. Ignoring the need to show the product in color, the second advertiser elected to use 20-second and 30-second television spots. With *about the same budget* he was able approximately to double the amount of exposure against the primary target group. (Emphasis added.)

The gamble on greater exposure at the sacrifice of a more dramatic creative approach paid off. . . . Field research revealed that consumer familiarity with the advertising campaign (for Brand A) was low, though it was well liked by those who claimed to have seen it. Most distressing, many who claimed familiarity with it actually attributed Brand A copy to Brand B. Obviously, the more frequent repetition of the Brand B name had enabled it to gain a substantially greater *share of mind*—a critical factor in the marketplace.[5]

Jones goes on to say, "The relative importance of creative impact through expensive space or time units versus greater exposure through less costly units must be resolved on the basis of judgment, experience, and a full awareness of the media alternatives."

Sales Promotion

Sales promotion, often referred to as merchandising, includes point-of-purchase display, sampling, coupons, contests, sweepstakes, cents-off packs, self-liquidating premiums, trade deals, and other selling aids.[6] Some forms of sales promotion have obvious media implications, especially in terms of selecting media types.

Coupons, often made available to consumers, can be redeemed for price reduction, cash, or merchandise. Because you cannot clip a coupon from a broadcast ad or a billboard, couponing efforts require magazines, newspapers, free standing inserts or direct mail unless the package is used for coupon distribution.

Occasionally marketers employ sampling as a form of sales promotion, a technique through which samples of the product are distributed to selected prospects. When it is not possible or desirable to distribute samples through sales people or retailers, direct mail must usually be relied upon to do the job.

Contests and sweepstakes offering prizes to entrants can be excellent tools for gaining consumer involvement. A contest generally requires that some task be performed by the entrant, such as telling, in 25 words or less, why he or she likes the product; a sweepstakes is based purely on chance and requires no skill on the part of the entrant. Rules for contests are often too complex to be announced on radio or television and therefore can be more practically communicated via print media or direct mail.

Besides physical media requirements, such as needing a printed page on which to put a coupon, the two most important determinants of what media type should be used to explain a promotion are (1) the complexity of the promotion and (2) the purpose of the promotion. The more complex the promotion, the more likely that it will not be economically practical to explain the promotion within the time constraints imposed by broadcast media. However, using broadcast to ask consumers to "pick up the rules at your supermarket" may be an acceptable alternative.

The purpose of the promotion is an important consideration because, in many cases, the primary goal of the promotion is something other than getting people to participate. Promotions are often used to gain brand awareness, increase consumer interest, achieve trade cooperation, or expose the brand to new market segments. These promotions may be announced in broadcast media since the details or rules are not the key communication points.

Personal Selling

The extent to which personal selling is employed in the marketer's promotion mix has an overall effect on the opportunity to use advertising media. Advertising is used when it is not economically feasible to use personal selling alone to move the product through the distribution channel; thus, a greater degree of emphasis on personal selling reduces the advertising-to-sales ratio and may result in a smaller advertising budget. Budget constraints so imposed may preclude the substantial investment required for network television, for example. On the other hand, less emphasis on personal selling increases the opportunity to buy advertising time and space. Moreover, in territories where a sales force is weak or does not exist, a push or pull advertising strategy may be heavily relied upon, increasing the opportunity to use trade or consumer media, respectively.

Packaging

Packaging has a dual role in the marketing mix; it is a product component and acts as a promotional tool as well. This dual role can be illustrated by an ordinary box of facial tissues. The box, once its top has been removed, functions as a tissue holder and is thus a part of the product. But the box is also a promotional device as it sits on the grocery shelf and visually displays the brand name. In addition, when a marketing objective is to increase consumption by present users of the product, the package or label can be used to reach these users with a coupon or redemption offer.

Packaging as a product dimension affects media planning when the package has an innovative feature of communication importance. Whether the feature is easy or hard to communicate will influence the media type selection. Many package innovations must be communicated by demonstration in the television medium.

To assess the media implications of packaging as a promotional device, we must determine the importance of the package's visual aspects. A crucial factor is the role of the package at the point of purchase. In a self-service situation, such as we typically find in grocery stores, the package must help sell the product. Advertisers whose products are distributed through self-service retail outlets usually strive to enhance package identification among consumers. Selection of media type is certainly influenced, since package identification cannot be achieved through the radio medium but can be accomplished through most other media with varying degrees of effectiveness.

There is a strong continuing trend toward self-service among today's retailers. By increasing the significance of packaging's promotional role, this trend will also make packaging considerations more important to media planners.

The Marketing Mix as a System

As you have been reading about the different components of the marketing mix, it is hoped you have become aware that much interaction exists between these components. You have seen that the structure of the distribution channel is closely tied together with push-pull promotion decisions. We have also discussed the interplay between product characteristics and advertising objectives, which in turn interact with the media plan. Examples of mix interaction are indeed numerous, and the two just cited are perhaps more obvious than many of the others.

We therefore remind you that the marketing mix is an integrated system composed of interrelated parts and, although we have by necessity discussed each part separately, you should recognize that a decision in any area of the mix is likely to affect other areas, including media planning.

How Uncontrollable Variables Affect the Environment for Media Decisions

Recall from Chapter 1 and Figure 1.1 that uncontrollable variables must be taken into account by the media planner throughout the entire decision making process. These constraints can have a profound effect on the outcome of the media effort and media planners should be aware of them.

Internal Uncontrollable Variables

It is apparent that most variables in the marketing mix are beyond the control of the media planner. In addition to the constraints imposed by these variables and by the size of the advertising budget, media planning is further constrained by another set of factors within the firm: company policy and company image.

Although a prestigious company may encourage its media planners to use prestigious media types (notably television), the planner feels the influence of company policy and image primarily at the level of choosing media vehicles. To illustrate, consider that a company enjoying a wholesome family-oriented image would refrain from advertising in a publication which contains editorial content of little socially redeeming value, no matter how well the publication's audience profile matches the product's target market. The media planner may have to settle for a less perfect match to keep the company's advertising in line with corporate policy and an image that has taken years to establish.

External Uncontrollable Variables

Of the many uncontrollable variables external to the firm that affect marketing operations, at least five of these variables directly affect media planning: (1) competitive efforts, (2) economic conditions, (3) the legal and cultural environment, (4) weather/cataclysmic conditions/ acts of God, and (5) media environment.

Competitive Efforts. Amid the clutter of advertising messages pouring forth from the media, any given message must compete with numerous others for the consumer's attention. Although the media planner is concerned with the overall quantity of messages in a medium, he or she is more directly concerned with the quantity of messages for competing products.

The way that competitive efforts affect media selection is largely determined by whether you are advertising a differentiated, superior product or an undifferentiated "me-too" product. Suppose, for instance, that you are buying media for a major brand of coffee and find two magazines equally attractive as media buys in terms of quantitative considerations. If Magazine A has no other coffee ads, but four full pages in Magazine B have been bought by other companies to advertise coffee, Magazine A becomes the better buy because direct competition between messages is minimized. The impact and memorability of a message for a "me-too" brand of coffee is bound to be diluted when competing with several messages for nearly identical products.

However, what if you are buying media for a stereo component system that offers unique design and superior sound and engineering? Then it may be wise to select a vehicle that carries directly competing messages. As the consumer shops in the vehicle by comparing your product to those advertised in competing messages, the superiority of your product may become more apparent to the consumer.

Other factors that should be considered include avoiding creative approaches similar to competitors. From the standpoint of wanting to minimize confusion among consumers, it is desirable to avoid placing an ad in a vehicle or medium that carries a competitive ad that is similar to yours in appearance or format.

Sometimes, however, a judgment is made—occasionally based on research—that your creative approach is more persuasive or has better recall than the approach of your competitor; or that a competitor's positive attributes are credited to your product in consumers' minds.

Provisions should also be made in the media plan to cope with competitive reactions, such as in the case of a new product, when a competitor starts distributing free samples to upset your product introduction. One such provision for products with good rates of repurchase, is to cover several purchase cycles (never just one) with the introductory effort. For example, if the average consumer repurchases your product every six weeks, then your introductory media effort should cover *at least* twelve weeks, or two purchase cycles.

Specific media selections can be dictated by competitive efforts Exclusive sponsorship, for example, can serve an advertiser by not only reaching a desired target market, but by blocking out all competitors and therefore forcing them into less effective media. This is most visible in televised sporting events.

In suggesting that competitive efforts are of primary importance in deciding how much to spend and in what media to spend it, the advertising literature occasionally implies that what works for your competitors will work for you. Don't accept this principle without an understanding of its limitations. The needs of every advertiser—even within the same industry—are uniquely different and usually require different combinations of media alternatives to insure that those needs are adequately fulfilled.

Economic Conditions. In addition to affecting the budget that will be appropriated for media expenditures, economic conditions influence media prices and therefore affect the amount of time or space that each dollar in that budget can buy. Taking this a step further, certain economic problems may tend to make one media type more expensive relative to others. During an economic recession, for example, suppose that the level of production in the paper industry declines to a point where the demand for paper exceeds the supply. A likely result is that the price of paper will go up. In order to cover these additional costs, newspapers and magazines may increase their advertising rates. Relative to newspapers and magazines, broadcast media (since they are not significantly affected by paper prices) now become less expensive buys than they were before the downturn in the economy.

Media planning may be further influenced by economic conditions in certain markets. In one market area, for example, an unusually high unemployment rate has lowered per capita disposable income. Since the net effect of this is a somewhat reduced opportunity to sell products to people in that market, media planners may decide to buy less space in that market's newspapers and channel the money into space in the newspapers of more economically sound markets where consumers have a better ability to pay.

Legal and Cultural Environment. Theoretically, our law is a reflection of our culture and society, so here the influences of culture and the law are treated together. As our cultural environment and moral standards change, the law changes to accommodate society's beliefs as

to what is proper or desirable. Products that were not allowed to advertise in the mass media even a few years ago are now able to appeal to
millions through the air waves and the printed word. Feminine hygiene
deodorant is such a product. By the same token, alcoholic beverages recently have been under attack by several groups wanting it barred from
advertising in the mass media.

The legal environment for media planning consists of two forces: the
law itself and the rules established by self-regulating bodies within the
advertising industry. An example of law affecting media planning is
the Public Health Cigarette Smoking Act of 1971. Media planners for
cigarette advertising cannot consider broadcast media in evaluating alternatives because this law bans the advertising of cigarettes from radio
and television. And, of course, products that are themselves illegal in
some states (such as fireworks) cannot be advertised in those states.

Even more constraining in scope are the regulations imposed from
within the advertising industry, especially by the media themselves. A
number of media vehicles—including individual newspapers, magazines, radio and television stations—have developed codes and
standards that limit the types of products they will accept for advertising. One of the most notable examples here is *Good Housekeeping*
magazine. Their consumer policy reads, in part, as follows:

> Since 1885 *Good Housekeeping* has provided unique consumer
> education and consumer protection. The magazine maintains high
> levels of good taste and exercises strict editorial judgments in the
> consideration of products it will accept for advertising and in
> reviewing the advertising copy it publishes. These judgments comprise
> the basis of the *Good Housekeeping* Consumers' Refund or
> Replacement Policy.
>
> Source: Reprinted by permission from Good Housekeeping, *copyright*
> © *by The Hearst Corporation*

Keep in mind that in addition to regulations barring the advertising
of specific products, much broader regulations exist pertaining to the
ways in which products are presented. Accordingly, media planners
may be further limited in their choices if message content does not conform to high standards of social acceptability.

Weather/Cataclysmic Conditions/Acts of God. Surely you will agree
that there are few variables as uncontrollable as the nature of the physical environment itself. But how these factors affect media planning
may not be readily apparent.

Seasonal skews in the sales curve of many products are directly correlated with the weather. Air conditioners, insecticides, snowmobiles, golf equipment, and female shaving cream and depilatories are but a few examples. Suppose you are planning media for a seasonal product, such as a brand of suntan lotion that has national distribution. In scheduling the advertising by geographic region, it is likely that in April—because of climatic conditions—you would want to begin buying substantially more time and space in the southwestern region, while perhaps waiting until the end of May to increase expenditures in the upper midwest.

In addition to its effect on media scheduling, weather may also present special opportunities to select certain types of media. A department store in Minneapolis, for example, may find it advantageous during a bitter January cold wave to buy radio time and use it to urge customers to shop by telephone or by mail.

Weather may affect the degree of interest with which a program is watched or a magazine is read. Boating and golf magazines, for example, are read with more interest in warmer months when there is greater opportunity for its readers to get outdoors and actively pursue their recreational interests. This may be a significant qualitative consideration in assessing the potential effectiveness of a media buy.

Other uncontrollable aspects of the physical environment are cataclysmic conditions and acts of God. Consider, for example, that airlines frequently adopt a policy of cancelling scheduled advertising, especially in broadcast media and newspapers, immediately following an airline tragedy. When the Challenger space shuttle disaster occurred in early 1986, the three major television networks, ABC, CBS, NBC, removed all pre-scheduled commercials from their broadcasts (at an estimated loss of $9 million in revenues). The commercials that were supposed to run were either re-scheduled in later programs or eliminated from the media plan. Likewise, a media planner must be alert to react to special conditions in markets which may be struck by natural disasters such as floods, tornadoes, earthquakes, or volcanos.

Media Environment. It is impossible for an advertiser to completely control the fate of an ad once it is in the hands of the media.

In print media, for example, what if a coupon for another product is backed up to your ad? When the coupon is clipped, your ad and perhaps even *your* coupon will be mutilated. This is unlikely to occur in certain publications, of course; and there is usually recourse—a discount or a free re-run of your ad—but that particular placement could be considered a "loss."

The environment within a particular media vehicle can become unfavorable for an ad that is placed adjacent to editorial material which may be detrimental to the image of the advertised product. In print, a cigarette manufacturer would not want its ad to run next to an article about lung cancer, just as a bank would not want its ad on the same newspaper page that has an account of yesterday's robbery of that bank. In broadcast media, the environment for an ad may likewise deteriorate if the ad is run adjacent to news programs or documentaries which treat subjects that may lead consumer attitudes in a direction unfavorable to the advertised product.

Uncontrollable Constraints as Opportunities

The innovative media planner will not be content to simply accept uncontrollable constraints; rather, he or she will investigate ways of using them to the best advantage.

Consider that radio stations imposing abnormal constraints on the amount of advertising carried per hour offer the opportunity to place advertising in a relatively uncluttered environment. Such a setting may be especially helpful, for example, in the case of a restauranteur who wants to convey the relaxing, get-away-from-it-all atmosphere of his eatery. There are also opportunities inherent in purchasing time from television stations that are willing to maintain below-average levels of advertising clutter.

Although economic conditions are another element beyond advertisers' control, an undesirable economic picture does not always dictate that the media effort should be curtailed. An economic recession may even provide an opportunity to gain widespread awareness for an advertiser who decides to maintain or heavy-up an effort while competitors decrease their advertising activity.

Environmental situations such as energy shortages may also harbor opportunities for the alert media planner. Aggressive public utilities did not slash their media budgets when the energy crisis entered the mainstream of American concerns. Instead, they used their advertising time and space to communicate ideas on energy conservation.

In the media environment as well, uncontrollable constraints may be converted into advantages by prudent advertisers. Consider the constraint imposed by *Good Housekeeping's* policy of accepting ads only for products which the magazine feels are of unquestionable integrity. For advertisers whose products live up to that standard, the *Good Housekeeping* "constraint" becomes an opportunity to advertise in an environment that is characterized by relatively high consumer trust.

Looking for a positive side to uncontrollable constraints is a challenge that, when met, can point the way to unique, successful advertising and media strategies.

Summary

This chapter was devoted to explaining the idea with which it began: media problems are marketing problems. You have seen that media planners cannot ignore the important influences of different elements of the marketing mix, including product characteristics, distribution channels, pricing strategy, promotion, and packaging, each of which provides inputs for media decisions.

Emphasis was placed on the significant effects which the promotion mix has on media planning, for promotion is the element of the marketing plan that is closest to the media decision maker. The media plan ultimately depends upon the nature of activities within the areas of sales promotion, personal selling and advertising itself, including advertising objectives, positioning strategy, and message content.

The media implications of company policy and company image were also discussed. In addition to having the responsibility of using media that are consistent with company policy and image, the media planner must also contend with several uncontrollable variables that are external to the firm, including competitive efforts, economic conditions, the legal and cultural environment, weather, cataclysmic conditions, acts of God, and media environment. Although these variables may be viewed as constraints, the alert media planner often sees them as opportunities.

Before the influence of uncontrollable variables was discussed, it was necessary to review the concept of the marketing mix as an integrated system of interrelated parts. The system is such that decisions in one area of the mix tend to affect its other areas. Each component of the marketing mix system interacts to collectively move the product to consumers in a defined target market. Defining the target market is the subject of the next chapter.

Endnotes

1. For further discussion of product life cycle, see a basic marketing textbook; for example, David L. Kurtz and Louis E. Boone, *Marketing,* 2nd edition (Chicago: The Dryden Press, 1984), pp. 270-280.

2. Jack Z. Sissors and Jim Surmanek, *Advertising Media Planning,* 2nd edition (Lincolnwood: Crain Books/NTC Business Books, 1982), p. 124.

3. See David L. Kurtz and Louis E. Boone, *Marketing,* 2nd edition (Chicago: The Dryden Press, 1984), pp. 447-451.

4. For additional discussion of the positioning concept, see David L. Kurtz and Louis E. Boone, *Marketing,* 2nd edition (Chicago: The Dryden Press, 1984), p. 598; and Leo Bogart, *Strategy in Advertising,* 2nd edition (Lincolnwood: Crain Books/NTC Business Books, 1984), pp. 237-238.

5. Richard P. Jones, ''Media Planning,'' appearing in Roger Barton, ed., *Handbook of Advertising Management* (McGraw-Hill Book Co., New York, 1970), pp. 7-8.

6. A variety of sales promotion techniques are explained and illustrated in Don E. Schultz and William A. Robinson, *Sales Promotion Essentials* (Lincolnwood: Crain Books/NTC Business Books, 1982).

Chapter Three

Target Market Definition and Media-Market Matching

A single marketer cannot satisfy all the wants and needs of every consumer; nor are the advertiser's products designed for use by everyone. To do an efficient marketing job, marketers must define a target group of consumers as the most likely prospects for purchasing their products.

Marketing Plans Revolve Around Defined Markets

In the last chapter, you saw that the marketing plan provides a framework in which media decisions are made. And each area of the marketing mix is intimately connected with a defined target market. The product itself is tailored to that market. Distribution works to get that product to the right place at the right time, making it readily available to the right people. Pricing decisions must be made in light of what consumers in the target market are willing and able to pay; conversely, a product's price range may be an important determinant of how the target market is defined. Within the promotion mix, advertising must communicate with the right people—the consumers in the defined target market—as a catalyst for selling to those whose needs or wants can best be satisfied by the advertiser's brand. It is here that the media planner comes to the fore, because it is his or her job to see that the marketing message is delivered to the target market as defined in the marketing plan. In some instances, the media planner's analysis and interpretation of available data may be instrumental in arriving at a target market definition.

Matching Markets and Media

Once the media planner is given a target market definition, what does he or she do with it? The principle underlying efficient use of advertising time and space is matching markets and media—that is, the media planner tries to invest advertising dollars in those media vehicles having audiences that closely parallel the description of the target market. The better the match, the less money wasted on delivering messages to consumers for whom the product was not intended in the first place.

Parameters for Defining the Target Market

To get a better feel for what the media planner works with in matching markets and media, let us examine the various ways in which advertisers define target markets. Once these parameters for target definition have been reviewed, we will assess their significance in media decision-making.

Target markets may be defined in terms of any or all of three types of variables: (1) demographic, (2) sociopsychological, and (3) product usage.

Demographics

Demographic variables include age, sex, income, occupation, education, family life cycle (marital status and age of children), family size, race, religion, geographic region, county size, and locality. Although these variables are largely self-explanatory, it is helpful to be familiar with the specific breakdowns typically found within each category. Bear in mind that breakdowns vary from one research service to the next (see Table 3.1).

It is not an absolute necessity that marketers use all of these demographic variables in defining a target market. Each time another demographic variable is added to the definition, the target narrows in scope. The desirable balance between defining targets too broadly or too narrowly is just this: the target should be defined specifically enough so that the media planner will know what type of audience to look for in making media comparisons, but should not be defined so narrowly that a significant number of real prospects are excluded from the target. Figure 3.1 shows what happens to the scope of the target as additional demographic characteristics are added to a target market definition.

Table 3.1
Major Demographic Variables and Suggested Breakdowns

Variable	Typical Breakdown
Age	Under 6, 6-11, 12-17, 18-24, 25-34, 35-44, 45-54, 55-64, 65+
Sex	Male, female
Income	Under $10,000, $10,000-$14,999, $15,000-$19,999, $20,000-$24,999, $25,000-$34,999, $35,000-$49,999, $50,000-$74,999, $75,000+
Education	Grade school or less; some high school; graduated high school; some college; graduated college
Occupation	Professional and technical; managers, officials, and proprietors; clerical, sales; craftworkers, supervisors; operatives; farmers; retired; students; housewives; unemployed
Family size	1-2, 3-4, 5+
Family life cycle	Young, single; young, married, no children; young, married, youngest child under 6; young, married, youngest child 6 or over; older, married, with children; older, married, no children under 18; older, single; other
Religion	Catholic, Protestant, Jewish, other
Race	White, Black, other
Geographic Region	Northeast; East Central; West Central; South; Pacific
County Size	A; B; C; D (A.C. Nielsen Company)
Locality	Metro central city; metro suburban; non metro

For a discussion of the variables and breakdowns, see S. Watson Dunn and Arnold M. Barban, *Advertising: Its Role in Modern Marketing,* 6th edition (Hinsdale, Ill.: Dryden Press, 1986), pp. 293-301.

It is important at this point to review the concept of market segmentation, which has been defined as "the process of dividing the total market into several relatively homogeneous groups."[1] This definition suggests that the marketer tailors the product to satisfy a segment of the market that can be described in terms of the breakdowns within each demographic variable, or in terms of the other target market parameters mentioned thus far. It is the media planner's job to deliver the marketing message to consumers in that segment.

Figure 3.1

The Absolute Size of a Target Market Changes As Additional Variables Are Added to the Definition

Note that when only *one* variable is used to define the target, 80,052,000 individuals are included; with three variables, the size is 23,020,000; seven variables results in a target size of 6,306,000.

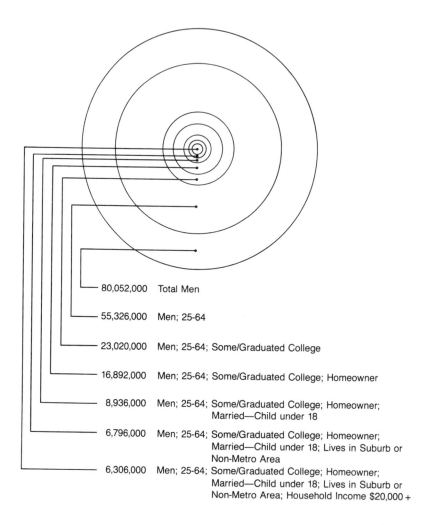

80,052,000	Total Men	
55,326,000	Men; 25-64	
23,020,000	Men; 25-64; Some/Graduated College	
16,892,000	Men; 25-64; Some/Graduated College; Homeowner	
8,936,000	Men; 25-64; Some/Graduated College; Homeowner; Married—Child under 18	
6,796,000	Men; 25-64; Some/Graduated College; Homeowner; Married—Child under 18; Lives in Suburb or Non-Metro Area	
6,306,000	Men; 25-64; Some/Graduated College; Homeowner; Married—Child under 18; Lives in Suburb or Non-Metro Area; Household Income $20,000 +	

Source: 1985 SMRB Study of Media & Markets

Sociopsychological Variables

Demographically, you may be dealing with a consumer who is a 35-44 year old male with a college degree and an annual income in the $35,000-$49,999 category, but this type of description certainly isn't all that can be said about this consumer. There are thousands of American consumers matching this demographic description, but by adding another dimension to target market definition—a sociopsychological dimension—we find that different consumers within this same segment may have very different values and attitudes, as well as different living patterns.

Under the sociopsychological umbrella are *psychographics* and *life-style,* both of which have been gaining popularity as parameters within which target markets can be defined. Psychographics are measures of consumer attitudes, interests, and opinions, and are used to classify consumers in terms of personality characteristics borrowed from the field of social psychology. Examples of such characteristics are leadership, independence, need achievement, compulsiveness, gregariousness, aggressiveness, and conformity.

In addition to helping the media planner, psychographics may prove to be essential information in order for the copywriter to understand the buyer's psyche. The buying style definitions such as those provided by a syndicated research service, as shown in Figure 3.2, can lead the writer to select more meaningful communication alternatives through knowledge of whether, for example, the buyer is "brand loyal" vs. "impulsive" or "conformist" vs. "experimenter."

Life-style is the unique way a person sees him- or herself in relation to work, leisure activities, and buying habits. It is a manifestation of attitudes and interests interacting with the cultural environment. The consumer's style of day-to-day living becomes visible through this interaction encompassing such things as how leisure time is used, what type of entertainment is enjoyed, and the extent of community involvement.

One particular life-style segmentation system is known as VALS—Values And Life-Styles—and was developed by SRI International (Stanford Research Institute). This system identifies three broad groups of consumers—the *need-driven,* the *outer-directed,* and the *inner-directed.* These three broad categories are further divided into a total of

Figure 3.2

PSYCHOGRAPHIC DEFINITIONS

Buying Style
Classification of Buying Style is based on self-ratings with respect to statements on a five-point scale
in which 1 = "agree a lot" and 2 = "agree a little." The statements and the scale points used to define
the classifications are as follows:

Ad Believer: In general advertising presents a true picture of the products of well known companies	1,2
Brand Loyal: I always look for the name of the manufacturer on the package	1
Cautious: I do not buy unknown brands merely to save money	1
Conformists: I prefer to buy things that my friends or neighbors would approve of	1,2
Ecologists: All products that pollute the environment should be banned	1
Economy-Minded: I shop around a lot to take advantage of specials or bargains	1
Experimenters: I like to change brands often for the sake of variety and novelty	1,2
Impulsive: When in the store, I often buy an item on the spur of the moment	1
Planners: I generally plan far ahead to buy expensive items such as automobiles	1
Style Conscious: I try to keep abreast of changes in styles and fashions	1

Source: 1985 SMRB Study of Media & Markets

nine VALS types (see figure 3.3). The broad groups are described as follows:[2]

Need-Driven: Money-restricted consumers who are struggling just to buy the basics.

Outer-Directed: A diverse group whose behavior is strongly influenced by other people's opinions.

Inner-Directed: An affluent population noted for being individualistic and experimental in living patterns, and having a high sense of social responsibility.

Another category, **Integrated,** is separate from the other three, and includes a very small segment of the population that combines the power of outer-directedness with the sensitivity of inner-directedness.

To realize the importance of the sociopsychological dimension, consider two consumers from the very same demographic market segment. (Let's use the same example we used previously: male, age 35-44, college graduate, income $35,000-$49,999.) Consumer A is an

Figure 3.2 (Cont.)

Self-Concept

Classification of Self-Concept is based on self-ratings with respect to groups of adjectives on a five-point scale in which 1 = "agree a lot" and 2 = "agree a little." The adjectives and the scale-points used to define the classifications are as follows:

Affectionate:	passionate, loving, romantic	1
Amicable:	Amiable, affable, benevolent	1
Awkward:	absent-minded, forgetful, careless	1,2
Brave:	courageous, daring, adventuresome	1,2
Broadminded:	open-minded, liberal, tolerant	1
Creative:	inventive, imaginative, artistic	1
Dominating:	authoritarian, demanding, aggressive	1,2
Efficient:	organized, diligent, thorough	1
Egocentric:	vain, self-centered, narcissistic	1,2
Frank:	straightforward, outspoken, candid	1
Funny:	humorous, amusing, witty	1
Intelligent:	smart, bright, well-informed	1
Kind:	good-hearted, warm-hearted, sincere	1
Refined:	gracious, sophisticated, dignified	1,2
Reserved:	conservative, quiet, conventional	1
Self-Assured:	confident, self-sufficient, secure	1
Sociable:	friendly, cheerful, likeable	1
Stubborn:	hardheaded, headstrong, obstinate	1,2
Tense:	nervous, high-strung, excitable	1,2
Trustworthy:	competent, reliable, responsible	1

Source: 1985 SMRB Study of Media & Markets

extroverted, aggressive leader in most everything he does. He is independent, ambitious, and feels little need to conform to the behavior of others. He is intensely involved in his work and has relatively little leisure time, but travels a lot on business.

Consumer B, from the same demographic segment, is rather shy and introverted and thus much more comfortable as a follower than as a leader. He depends heavily on other people and readily conforms to the behavioral norms found among his peers. He works little overtime and regularly enjoys camping, fishing, and boating.

The point of this example should be clear: these two consumers, although their demographic characteristics are very similar, cannot be reached with equal effectiveness by the same advertising media or the same message content.

Yet the use of psychographics should not be overstressed. While in many cases marketers look to these characteristics for a more descriptive definition of whose needs their product can satisfy, some dangers are inherent in depending solely on psychographics.

In a study done by the Newspaper Advertising Bureau, it was found that psychographics were least useful for products that enjoy

Figure 3.3

The VALS Typology

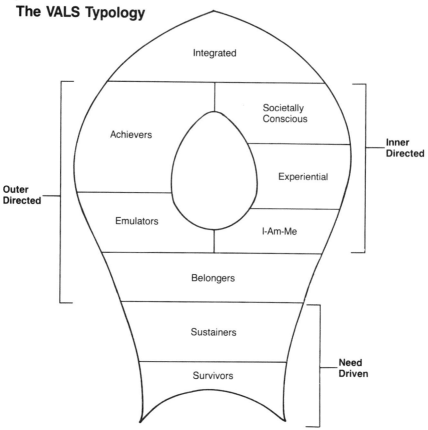

Source: Values and Lifestyles (VALS) Program
SRI International, Menlo Park, CA

almost universal use, such as toothpaste, but the study did show distinctive profiles for products and services with limited use (for example, air travel and alcoholic beverages).[3] The study warned that psychographic analysis is of minimal use in selecting media unless the product or the media are highly specialized. Sissors and Surmanek make the following observation:

> ...psychographics can be useful in media planning when certain conditions are met. If a market has been indentified demographically, yet there is reason to believe that the demographics do not segment the market precisely, then psychographic analysis may provide new dimensions of the target audience. If such new dimensions are found, however, it is important also to have available an analysis that shows

which alternative media reach large numbers of the psychographic categories that are shown to be important for the given brand. This may be difficult, because syndicated research services such as Simmons provide only a limited analysis of psychographic categories. It may mean that the planner will require custom-made research in order to find which alternative media reach the required psychographic categories.[4]

Product Usage Variables

Marketers often attempt to identify targets based on levels of product usage. Four volume segments are generally considered: heavy users, medium users, light users, and non-users. Product usage variables are especially useful to those marketers whose objectives call for increasing consumption among present customers or increasing brand share within the present market.

While it is often tempting to concentrate on the heavy user—since his or her propensity to consume is greatest—it is important to avoid segmenting the market too narrowly by including heavy users only. In the non-user segment, there may be a substantial number of potential users who can be converted into customers through promotion. It may also be worthwhile to give light users some good reasons to consume more of the product. Advertisements stressing new uses of a product are often a means to that end.

There are no hard-and-fast rules that indicate whether to pursue heavy users, light users, or non-users. The marketing situation, including industry growth and the brand's position in the marketplace, is the best overall guide to targeting decisions based on product usage.

In addition to examining product usage segments, the media planner may also find it useful to explore *brand* usage segments (as opposed to product usage levels). Four segments which best describe *how* a brand is used relative to competing brands are frequently referred to as: sole users (use your brand only), primary users (use your brand mostly but also use other brands), secondary users (use your brand sometimes but use others more often), and non-users (use the product but not your brand). The interaction between brand usage and product usage levels represents an exciting dimension in approaching target market definition and will give the media planner a deeper understanding of the advertising task relative to competition. It is hoped that interaction will become less difficult to grasp as research services become even more sophisticated.

Applying the Target Market Definition to Media Decisions

Currently, the three basic ways of defining the target markets just reviewed cannot be applied to media decisions with the same degree of utility. Two key considerations in deciding which approach to use are the availability of information and how such information relates to media usage. Target markets should be defined in the same terms as media audiences if the media planner is to avoid having to compare apples and oranges when matching markets and media.

Currently, demographic target descriptions—as well as those based on product usage levels—tend to be more useful than sociopsychological descriptions. This is because of the focus of syndicated research services and media-sponsored studies. Sociopsychological analyses of audiences can often be obtained only through time-consuming and costly primary research; yet, this is not to say that such research is not a worthwhile investment.

It is a common practice for media planners to use demographics in conjunction with product usage data in searching for an optimal media-market match. After examining combinations of data describing product usage by demographic categories, provided by syndicated services such as Simmons Market Research Bureau (SMRB) and Mediamark Research Inc. (MRI), we will discuss how the final connection is made between the target market definition and selected media audiences. (Although SMRB and MRI provide a basis for this discussion of syndicated services, the important point is not the existence of these two organizations in particular; rather, the key idea is that the kinds of information now provided by these services is likely to be available in one form or another.)

Simmons Market Research Bureau (SMRB) and Mediamark Research Inc. (MRI)

Within product categories, data from SMRB and MRI show demographic characteristics and media usage for varying levels of product use. Brand consumption within a product category is also reported in many cases.

Figure 3.4 is an excerpt from a SMRB report on the product category "light/low calorie domestic beer" and shows adult usage by heavy, medium, and light users, as well as among all users. The time frame for the consumption of low calorie beer is defined to be "usage in the last 7 days," and the various degrees of usage are shown as:

Heavy users: 5 or more cans or bottles of light/low calorie beer in last 7 days

Medium users: 2 to 4 cans/bottles

Light users: 1 or less can/bottle

Let's look further at Figure 3.4 in terms of just one demographic characteristic—for example, census regions (of which there are four: Northeast, North Central, South, and West). SMRB reports that there are more total low calorie beer users in the South than elsewhere—12,780,000 adults. Add to this information the number of "heavy" users and we have the following profile:

Census region	All users of low calorie beer	Heavy users of low calorie beer
Northeast	8,904,000	1,942,000
North Central	11,447,000	2,456,000
South	12,780,000	2,992,000
West	8,936,000	1,895,000
Totals	42,067,000	9,285,000

Yet, the larger number of low calorie beer users in the South must be balanced by the fact that Southerners are shown to be relatively below average in terms of consuming this product. This fact is reflected in the Index Numbers. For all users, the South has an index of 89—11 percent below the average (100-89 = 11%).

Figure 3.5, from SMRB, shows data for four specific brands of light beer and thus permits a planner to see the relationship between product users and brand users.

Figures 3.6 and 3.7 present product and brand information respectively as provided by the MRI syndicated research service. When both services report information for the same product class and brands, there can be notable differences in user patterns. Generally, such differences can be explained by such things as sample selection, when the studies were conducted, and interviewing techniques. Yet, unexplained differences occur nevertheless and present significant problems for the person using such information.

The SMRB and MRI data described above can be used for a variety of purposes, but their primary value is in allowing advertisers who have defined their target markets in terms of product usage to see who those users are in demographic terms. Then the advertiser can look for media audiences that have approximately the same demographic characteristics.

Figure 3.4

LIGHT/LOW CALORIE DOMESTIC BEER (IN CANS OR BOTTLES): USAGE IN LAST 7 DAYS (ADULTS)

	TOTAL U.S. '000	ALL USERS A '000	ALL USERS B %DOWN	ALL USERS C %ACROSS	ALL USERS D INDX	HEAVY USERS FIVE OR MORE A '000	HEAVY B %DOWN	HEAVY C %ACROSS	HEAVY D INDX	MEDIUM USERS TWO–FOUR A '000	MEDIUM B %DOWN	MEDIUM C %ACROSS	MEDIUM D INDX	LIGHT USERS ONE OR LESS A '000	LIGHT B %DOWN	LIGHT C %ACROSS	LIGHT D INDX
TOTAL ADULTS	169460	42067	100.0	24.8	100	9285	100.0	5.5	100	13916	100.0	8.2	100	18866	100.0	11.1	100
MALES	80052	21999	52.3	27.5	111	6203	66.8	7.7	141	7312	52.5	9.1	111	8484	45.0	10.6	95
FEMALES	89408	20068	47.7	22.4	90	3082	33.2	3.4	63	6604	47.5	7.4	90	10382	55.0	11.6	104
18 – 24	28611	8101	19.3	28.3	114	1947	21.0	6.8	124	2655	19.1	9.3	113	3500	18.6	12.2	110
25 – 34	40058	12518	29.8	31.2	126	2706	29.1	6.8	123	4022	28.9	10.0	122	5790	30.7	14.5	130
35 – 44	30132	8601	20.4	28.5	115	1676	18.1	5.6	102	2689	19.3	8.9	109	4236	22.5	14.1	126
45 – 54	22317	5042	12.0	22.6	91	1162	12.5	5.2	95	1896	13.6	8.5	103	1984	10.5	8.9	80
55 – 64	21993	4445	10.6	20.2	81	1037	11.2	4.7	86	1378	9.9	6.3	76	2030	10.8	9.2	83
65 OR OLDER	26350	3361	8.0	12.8	51	758	8.2	2.9	53	1277	9.2	4.8	59	1326	7.0	5.0	45
18 – 34	68669	20619	49.0	30.0	121	4653	50.1	6.8	124	6676	48.0	9.7	118	9290	49.2	13.5	122
18 – 49	110638	31926	75.9	28.9	116	6887	74.2	6.2	114	10403	74.8	9.4	115	14636	77.6	13.2	119
25 – 54	92507	26160	62.2	28.3	114	5544	59.7	6.0	109	8607	61.8	9.3	113	12010	63.7	13.0	117
35 – 49	41969	11307	26.9	26.9	109	2234	24.1	5.3	97	3727	26.8	8.9	108	5346	28.3	12.7	114
50 OR OLDER	58823	10141	24.1	17.2	69	2397	25.8	4.1	74	3513	25.2	6.0	73	4230	22.4	7.2	65
GRADUATED COLLEGE	28689	9143	21.7	31.9	128	1649	17.8	5.7	105	3178	22.8	11.1	135	4316	22.9	15.0	135
ATTENDED COLLEGE	29760	8763	20.8	29.4	119	1807	19.5	6.1	111	2667	19.2	9.0	109	4289	22.7	14.4	129
GRADUATED HIGH SCHOOL	67306	16730	39.8	24.9	100	3929	42.3	5.8	107	5289	38.0	7.9	96	7512	39.8	11.2	100
DID NOT GRADUATE HIGH SCHOOL	43705	7431	17.7	17.0	68	1899	20.5	4.3	79	2782	20.0	6.4	78	2749	14.6	6.3	56
EMPLOYED MALES	56764	17120	40.7	30.2	121	4733	51.0	8.3	152	5536	39.8	9.8	119	6851	36.3	12.1	108
EMPLOYED FEMALES	45302	12567	29.9	27.7	112	1775	19.1	3.9	72	4134	29.7	9.1	111	6658	35.3	14.7	132
EMPLOYED FULL-TIME	88763	26233	62.4	29.6	119	5847	63.0	6.6	120	8733	62.8	9.8	120	11653	61.8	13.1	118
EMPLOYED PART-TIME	13303	3454	8.2	26.0	105	661	7.1	5.0	91	937	6.7	7.0	86	1856	9.8	14.0	125
NOT EMPLOYED	67395	12379	29.4	18.4	74	2777	29.9	4.1	75	4246	30.5	6.3	77	5357	28.4	7.9	71
PROFESSIONAL/MANAGER	26470	9078	21.6	34.3	138	1798	19.4	6.8	124	2912	20.9	11.0	134	4368	23.2	16.5	148
TECH/CLERICAL/SALES	31679	9165	21.8	28.6	117	1460	15.7	4.6	84	3017	21.7	9.5	116	4688	24.8	14.8	133
PRECISION/CRAFT	12857	3543	8.4	27.6	111	1097	11.8	8.5	156	1158	8.3	9.0	110	1288	6.8	10.0	90
OTHER EMPLOYED	31060	7902	18.8	25.4	102	2154	23.2	6.9	127	2583	18.6	8.3	101	3165	16.8	10.2	92
SINGLE	36345	9993	23.8	27.5	111	2464	26.5	6.8	124	3316	23.8	9.1	111	4213	22.3	11.6	104
MARRIED	103592	25977	61.8	25.1	101	5301	57.1	5.1	93	8529	61.3	8.2	100	12147	64.4	11.7	105
DIVORCED/SEPARATED/WIDOWED	29524	6097	14.5	20.7	83	1520	16.4	5.1	94	2071	14.9	7.0	85	2506	13.3	13.3	76
PARENTS	58373	15976	38.0	27.4	110	3282	35.3	5.6	103	4945	35.5	8.5	103	7749	41.1	13.3	119
WHITE	147469	37913	90.1	25.7	104	8181	88.1	5.5	101	12288	88.3	8.3	101	17444	92.5	11.8	106
BLACK	18302	3339	7.9	18.2	73	900	9.7	4.9	90	1295	9.3	7.1	86	1144	6.1	6.3	56
OTHER	3689	814	1.9	22.1	89	204	2.2	5.5	101	333	2.4	9.0	110	278	1.5	7.5	68
NORTHEAST-CENSUS	36974	8904	21.2	24.1	97	1942	20.9	5.3	96	2772	19.9	7.5	91	4190	22.2	11.3	102
NORTH CENTRAL	42557	11447	27.2	26.9	108	2456	26.5	5.8	105	3254	23.4	7.6	93	5737	30.4	13.5	121
SOUTH	57701	12780	30.4	22.1	89	2992	32.2	5.2	95	4771	34.3	8.3	101	5017	26.6	8.7	78
WEST	32228	8936	21.2	27.7	112	1895	20.4	5.9	107	3119	22.4	9.7	118	3922	20.8	12.2	109

NORTHEAST-MKTG.	38103	20.5	22.6	91	1805	19.4	4.7	86	2854	20.5	7.5	91	3958	21.0	10.4	93
EAST CENTRAL	24421	14.9	25.6	103	1515	16.3	6.2	113	1839	13.2	7.5	92	2904	15.4	11.9	107
WEST CENTRAL	28542	19.0	28.0	113	1651	17.8	5.8	106	2375	17.1	8.3	101	3969	21.0	13.9	125
SOUTH	49737	27.3	23.1	93	2659	28.6	5.3	98	4212	30.3	8.5	103	4624	24.5	13.9	84
PACIFIC	28658	18.3	26.9	108	1655	17.8	5.8	105	2637	18.9	9.2	112	3410	18.1	11.9	107
COUNTY SIZE A	70260	41.1	24.6	99	3828	41.2	5.4	99	6189	44.5	8.8	107	7252	38.4	10.3	93
COUNTY SIZE B	50687	31.4	26.0	105	2738	29.5	5.9	99	4236	30.4	8.4	102	6218	33.0	12.3	110
COUNTY SIZE C	25733	15.7	25.6	103	1506	16.2	5.9	107	2061	14.8	8.0	98	3024	16.0	11.8	106
COUNTY SIZE D	22779	11.9	22.0	89	1212	13.1	5.3	97	1431	10.3	6.3	76	2372	12.6	10.4	94
METRO CENTRAL CITY	50827	29.8	24.7	99	2805	30.2	5.5	101	4325	31.1	8.5	104	5415	28.7	10.7	96
METRO SUBURBAN	77471	47.6	25.8	104	4205	45.3	5.4	99	6817	49.0	8.8	107	9001	47.7	11.6	104
NON METRO	41162	22.6	23.1	93	2274	24.5	5.5	101	2774	19.9	6.7	82	4450	23.6	10.8	97
TOP 5 ADI'S	36530	20.2	23.2	93	1775	19.1	4.9	89	2872	20.6	7.9	96	3829	20.3	10.5	94
TOP 10 ADI'S	50770	28.7	23.8	96	2690	29.0	4.9	89	4241	30.4	8.4	102	5149	27.3	10.1	91
TOP 20 ADI'S	72570	42.4	24.6	99	3777	40.7	5.2	95	6146	44.2	8.5	103	7912	41.9	10.9	98
HSHLD INC. $50,000 OR MORE	20974	15.2	30.6	123	1140	12.3	5.4	99	2309	16.6	11.0	134	2963	15.7	14.1	127
$40,000 OR MORE	38603	27.4	29.8	120	2057	22.2	5.3	97	4083	29.3	10.6	129	5370	28.5	13.9	125
$30,000 OR MORE	65657	56.5	29.5	119	3736	40.2	5.6	104	6521	46.9	9.9	121	9125	48.4	13.9	125
$25,000 OR MORE	82501	11.4	28.8	116	4610	49.6	6.2	102	7770	55.8	9.4	115	11385	60.3	13.8	124
$20,000 - $24,999	18523	8.8	25.9	104	1256	13.5	6.8	124	1407	10.1	7.6	92	2131	11.3	11.5	103
$15,000 - $19,999	15987	8.8	23.0	93	790	8.5	5.4	98	1240	8.9	7.8	94	1652	8.8	10.3	93
$10,000 - $14,999	23682	11.9	21.1	85	1269	13.7	5.4	98	1899	13.6	8.0	98	1829	9.7	7.7	69
UNDER $10,000	28767	11.5	16.8	68	1359	14.6	4.7	86	1601	11.5	5.6	68	1870	9.9	6.5	58
HOUSEHOLD OF 1 PERSON	20053	9.5	19.9	80	1145	12.3	5.7	104	1299	9.3	6.5	79	1547	8.2	7.7	69
2 PEOPLE	52536	30.2	24.2	97	2644	28.5	5.0	92	4186	30.1	8.0	97	5884	31.2	11.2	101
3 OR 4 PEOPLE	68502	44.6	27.4	110	4184	45.1	6.1	111	6285	45.2	9.2	112	8281	43.9	12.1	109
5 OR MORE PEOPLE	28369	15.7	24.6	94	1312	14.1	4.6	84	2146	15.4	7.6	92	3154	16.7	11.1	100
NO CHILD IN HSHLD	98374	55.4	23.7	95	5311	57.2	5.4	99	8008	57.5	8.1	99	9977	52.9	10.1	91
CHILD(REN) UNDER 2 YRS	10921	7.6	29.4	119	551	5.9	5.0	92	1020	7.3	9.3	114	1642	8.7	15.0	135
2 - 5 YEARS	25334	15.3	25.5	103	1318	14.2	6.3	115	2095	15.1	8.3	101	3044	16.1	12.0	108
6 - 11 YEARS	31780	20.3	26.8	108	2003	21.6	6.3	115	2800	20.1	8.8	107	3722	19.7	11.7	105
12 - 17 YEARS	35615	21.1	24.9	100	1910	20.6	5.4	98	2816	20.2	7.9	96	4155	22.0	11.7	105
RESIDENCE OWNED	118551	68.0	24.1	97	5782	62.3	4.9	89	9658	69.4	8.1	99	13172	69.8	11.1	100
VALUE: $60,000 OR MORE	59901	37.9	26.6	107	2958	31.9	4.9	90	5414	38.9	9.0	110	7564	40.1	12.6	113
VALUE: UNDER $60,000	58650	30.1	21.6	87	2823	30.4	4.8	88	4244	30.5	7.2	88	5608	29.7	9.6	86

SIMMONS MARKET RESEARCH BUREAU, INC. 1985

*A SINGLE ASTERISK IN THE COLUMN OR ROW TOTAL INDICATES THAT THE CORRESPONDING
PERCENTAGES DOWN (COLUMN) OR ACROSS (ROW) ARE SUBJECT TO SIGNIFICANT SAMPLING
VARIABILITY AND SHOULD BE USED WITH CAUTION
** A DOUBLE ASTERISK IN THE COLUMN OR ROW TOTAL INDICATES THAT THE CORRESPONDING
PERCENTAGES DOWN (COLUMN) OR ACROSS (ROW) ARE TOO UNSTABLE FOR RELIABLE USE THEY
ARE SHOWN FOR CONSISTENCY ONLY

Source: 1985 SMRB Study of Media & Markets

Figure 3.5

LIGHT/LOW CALORIE DOMESTIC BEER (IN CANS OR BOTTLES): BRANDS
(ADULTS)

	TOTAL U.S. '000	BUDWEISER LIGHT A '000	B DOWN %	C ACROSS %	D INDX	COORS LIGHT A '000	B DOWN %	C ACROSS %	D INDX	MICHELOB LIGHT A '000	B DOWN %	C ACROSS %	D INDX	MILLER LITE A '000	B DOWN %	C ACROSS %	D INDX
TOTAL ADULTS	169460	14643	100.0	8.6	100	10848	100.0	6.4	100	10189	100.0	6.0	100	19389	100.0	11.4	100
MALES	80052	7941	54.2	9.9	115	5953	54.9	7.4	116	5465	53.6	6.8	114	9832	50.7	12.3	107
FEMALES	89408	6702	45.8	7.5	87	4896	45.1	5.5	86	4724	46.4	5.3	88	9557	49.3	10.7	93
18 – 24	28611	3692	25.2	12.9	149	2438	22.5	8.5	133	2222	21.8	7.8	129	3778	19.5	13.2	115
25 – 34	40058	4479	30.6	11.2	129	3247	29.9	8.1	127	3328	32.7	8.3	138	6360	32.8	15.9	139
35 – 44	30132	2778	19.0	9.2	107	2340	21.6	7.8	121	2049	20.1	6.8	113	4125	21.3	13.7	120
45 – 54	22317	1483	10.1	6.6	77	1152	10.6	5.2	81	1106	10.9	5.0	82	2400	12.4	10.8	94
55 – 64	21993	1264	8.6	5.7	67	955	8.8	4.3	68	919	9.0	4.2	69	1549	8.0	7.0	62
65 OR OLDER	26350	947	6.5	3.6	42	716	6.6	2.7	42	566	5.6	2.1	36	1178	6.1	4.5	39
18 – 34	68669	8171	55.8	11.9	138	5685	52.4	8.3	129	5549	54.5	8.1	134	10137	52.3	14.8	129
18 – 49	110638	11795	80.6	10.7	123	8581	79.1	7.8	121	8246	80.9	7.5	124	15636	80.6	14.1	124
25 – 54	92507	8740	59.7	9.4	109	6739	62.1	7.3	114	6483	63.6	7.0	117	12885	66.5	13.9	122
35 – 49	41969	3624	24.7	8.6	100	2897	26.7	6.9	108	2697	26.5	6.4	107	5498	28.4	13.1	114
50 OR OLDER	58823	2848	19.4	4.8	56	2267	20.9	3.9	60	1943	19.1	3.3	55	3753	19.4	6.4	56
GRADUATED COLLEGE	28689	3330	22.7	11.6	134	2938	27.1	10.2	160	2607	25.6	9.1	151	4281	22.1	14.9	130
ATTENDED COLLEGE	29760	3369	23.0	11.3	131	2666	24.6	9.0	140	2584	25.4	8.7	144	4184	21.6	14.1	123
GRADUATED HIGH SCHOOL	67306	5612	38.3	8.3	96	3636	33.5	5.4	84	3603	35.4	5.4	89	8054	41.5	12.0	105
DID NOT GRADUATE HIGH SCHOOL	43705	2331	15.9	5.3	62	1608	14.8	3.7	57	1396	13.7	3.2	53	2870	14.8	6.6	57
EMPLOYED MALES	56764	6362	43.4	11.2	130	4786	44.1	8.4	132	4473	43.9	7.9	131	8251	42.6	14.5	127
EMPLOYED FEMALES	45302	4220	28.8	9.3	108	3373	31.1	7.4	116	3192	31.3	7.0	117	6343	32.7	14.0	122
EMPLOYED FULL-TIME	88763	9331	63.7	10.5	122	7204	66.4	8.1	127	6790	66.6	7.6	127	12941	66.7	14.6	127
EMPLOYED PART-TIME	13303	1250	8.5	9.4	109	954	8.8	7.2	112	875	8.6	6.6	109	1653	8.5	12.4	109
NOT EMPLOYED	67395	4061	27.7	6.0	70	2690	24.8	4.0	62	2524	24.8	3.7	62	4795	24.7	7.1	62
PROFESSIONAL/MANAGER	26470	3167	21.6	12.0	138	2878	26.5	10.9	170	2625	25.8	9.9	165	4258	22.0	16.1	141
TECH/CLERICAL/SALES	31679	2864	19.6	9.9	105	2343	21.6	7.9	123	2432	23.9	7.7	128	4901	25.3	15.5	135
PRECISION/CRAFT	12857	1270	8.7	9.9	114	1011	9.3	7.9	123	679	6.7	5.3	88	1766	9.1	13.7	120
OTHER EMPLOYED	31060	3282	22.4	10.6	122	1926	17.8	6.2	97	1930	18.9	6.2	103	3669	18.9	11.8	103
SINGLE	36345	3838	26.2	10.6	122	3045	28.1	8.1	131	2728	26.8	7.5	125	4824	24.9	13.3	116
MARRIED	103592	8747	59.7	8.4	98	6325	58.3	6.1	95	6238	61.2	6.0	100	11549	59.6	11.1	97
DIVORCED/SEPARATED/WIDOWED	29524	2057	14.0	7.0	81	1478	13.6	5.0	78	1223	12.0	4.1	69	3016	15.6	10.2	89
PARENTS	58373	5572	38.1	9.5	110	3885	35.8	6.7	104	4064	39.9	7.0	116	7817	40.3	13.4	117
WHITE	147469	13237	90.4	9.0	104	9654	89.0	6.5	102	9294	91.2	6.3	105	17699	91.3	12.0	105
BLACK	18302	1121	7.7	6.1	71	857	7.9	4.7	73	743	7.3	4.1	68	1431	7.4	7.8	68
OTHER	3689	285	1.9	7.7	89	337	3.1	9.1	143	152	1.5	4.1	69	260	1.3	7.0	62
NORTHEAST-CENSUS	36974	3013	20.6	8.1	94	408	3.8	1.1	17	2690	26.4	7.3	121	4328	22.3	11.7	102
NORTH CENTRAL	42557	3548	24.2	8.3	96	2419	22.3	5.7	89	2248	22.1	5.3	88	6264	32.3	14.7	129
SOUTH	57701	4053	27.7	7.0	81	4223	38.9	7.1	114	2908	28.5	5.0	84	5726	29.5	9.9	87
WEST	32228	4029	27.5	12.5	145	3799	35.0	11.8	184	2343	23.0	7.3	121	3071	15.8	9.5	83

	TOTAL	A '000	A %	A %	A IDX	B '000	B %	B %	B IDX	C '000	C %	C %	C IDX	D '000	D %	D %	D IDX
NORTHEAST-MKTG.	38103	3043	20.8	8.0	92	505	4.7	1.3	21	2681	26.3	7.0	117	4163	21.5	10.9	95
EAST CENTRAL	24421	1892	12.9	7.7	90	871	8.0	3.6	56	1599	15.7	6.5	109	3552	18.3	14.5	127
WEST CENTRAL	28542	2398	16.4	8.4	97	2393	22.1	8.4	131	1298	12.3	4.4	73	3949	20.4	13.8	121
SOUTH	49737	3706	25.3	7.5	86	3918	36.1	7.9	123	2608	25.6	5.2	87	5095	26.3	10.2	90
PACIFIC	28658	3604	24.6	12.6	146	3161	29.1	11.0	172	2044	20.1	7.1	119	2630	13.6	9.2	80
COUNTY SIZE A	70260	6023	41.1	8.6	99	4233	39.0	6.0	94	4516	44.3	6.4	107	7888	40.7	11.2	98
COUNTY SIZE B	50687	4575	31.2	9.0	104	3380	31.2	6.7	104	3216	31.6	6.3	106	6500	33.5	12.8	112
COUNTY SIZE C	25733	2299	15.7	8.9	103	1717	15.8	6.7	104	1660	16.3	6.5	107	2960	15.3	11.5	101
COUNTY SIZE D	22779	1746	11.9	7.7	89	1518	14.0	6.7	104	797	7.8	3.5	58	2041	10.5	9.0	78
METRO CENTRAL CITY	50827	4343	29.7	8.5	99	3838	35.4	7.6	118	3180	31.2	6.3	104	5919	30.5	11.6	102
METRO SUBURBAN	77471	7038	48.1	9.1	105	4393	40.5	5.7	89	4989	49.0	6.4	107	9409	48.5	12.1	106
NON METRO	41162	3261	22.3	7.9	92	2617	24.1	6.4	99	2021	19.8	4.9	82	4062	21.0	9.9	86
TOP 5 ADI'S	36530	3225	22.0	8.8	102	1801	16.6	4.9	77	2501	24.5	6.8	114	3625	18.7	9.9	87
TOP 10 ADI'S	50771	4424	30.2	8.7	101	2613	24.1	5.1	80	3466	34.0	6.8	114	5440	28.1	10.7	94
TOP 20 ADI'S	72570	6140	41.9	8.5	98	4160	38.3	5.7	90	4730	46.4	6.5	108	7910	40.8	10.9	95
HSHLD INC. $50,000 OR MORE	20974	2234	15.3	10.7	123	1722	15.9	8.2	128	2183	21.4	10.4	173	3038	15.7	14.5	127
$40,000 OR MORE	38603	4099	28.0	10.6	123	3208	29.6	8.3	130	3764	36.9	9.8	162	5456	28.1	14.1	124
$30,000 OR MORE	65657	6873	46.9	10.5	121	5397	49.8	8.2	128	5723	56.2	8.7	145	9290	47.9	14.1	124
$25,000 OR MORE	82501	8729	59.6	10.6	122	6328	58.3	7.7	120	6672	65.5	8.1	135	11518	59.4	14.0	122
$20,000 - $24,999	18523	1445	9.9	7.8	90	1355	12.5	7.3	114	873	8.6	4.7	78	2209	11.4	11.9	104
$15,000 - $19,999	15987	1278	8.7	8.0	93	868	8.0	5.4	85	800	7.9	5.0	83	1711	8.8	10.7	94
$10,000 - $14,999	23682	1570	10.7	6.6	77	1208	11.1	5.1	80	905	8.9	3.8	64	2125	11.0	9.0	78
UNDER $10,000	28767	1621	11.1	5.6	65	1090	10.0	3.8	59	940	9.2	3.3	54	1827	9.4	6.4	56
HOUSEHOLD OF 1 PERSON	20053	1234	8.4	6.2	71	1193	11.0	5.9	93	898	8.8	4.5	74	1849	9.5	9.2	81
2 PEOPLE	52536	4031	27.5	7.7	89	2803	25.8	5.3	83	2661	26.1	7.0	84	5910	30.5	11.2	98
3 OR 4 PEOPLE	68502	6717	45.9	9.8	113	5212	48.0	5.8	119	4796	47.1	7.0	116	8777	45.3	12.8	112
5 OR MORE PEOPLE	28369	2660	18.2	9.4	109	1641	15.1	5.8	90	1834	18.0	6.5	108	2853	14.7	10.1	88
NO CHILD IN HSHLD	98374	7821	53.4	8.0	92	6240	57.5	6.3	99	5427	53.3	5.5	92	10576	54.5	10.8	94
CHILD(REN) UNDER 2 YRS	10921	1421	9.7	13.0	151	820	7.6	7.5	117	956	9.4	8.8	146	1476	7.6	13.5	118
2 - 5 YEARS	25334	2365	16.2	9.3	108	1783	16.4	7.1	110	1768	17.4	7.0	116	2964	15.3	11.7	102
6 - 11 YEARS	31780	3158	21.6	9.9	115	2268	20.9	7.1	110	2178	21.4	6.9	114	3926	20.2	12.4	108
12 - 17 YEARS	35615	3124	21.3	8.8	102	1985	18.3	5.6	87	2163	21.2	6.1	101	4163	21.5	11.7	102
RESIDENCE OWNED	118551	9450	64.5	8.0	92	7055	65.0	6.0	93	6748	66.2	5.7	95	12714	65.6	10.7	94
VALUE: $60,000 OR MORE	59901	5737	39.2	9.6	111	4024	37.1	6.7	105	4537	44.5	7.6	126	6913	35.7	11.5	101
VALUE: UNDER $60,000	58650	3713	25.4	6.3	73	3031	27.9	5.2	81	2211	21.7	3.8	63	5801	29.9	9.9	86

SIMMONS MARKET RESEARCH BUREAU, INC. 1985.

*A SINGLE ASTERISK IN THE COLUMN OR ROW TOTAL INDICATES THAT THE CORRESPONDING PERCENTAGES DOWN (COLUMN) OR ACROSS (ROW) ARE SUBJECT TO SIGNIFICANT SAMPLING VARIABILITY AND SHOULD BE USED WITH CAUTION

** A DOUBLE ASTERISK IN THE COLUMN OR ROW TOTAL INDICATES THAT THE CORRESPONDING PERCENTAGES DOWN (COLUMN) OR ACROSS (ROW) ARE TOO UNSTABLE FOR RELIABLE USE THEY ARE SHOWN FOR CONSISTENCY ONLY

Source: 1985 SMRB Study of Media & Markets

Figure 3.6

110 LOW CALORIE DOMESTIC BEER

BASE: ADULTS	TOTAL U.S. '000	ALL A '000	B % DOWN	C % ACROSS	D INDEX	HEAVY MORE THAN 5 A '000	B % DOWN	C % ACROSS	D INDEX	MEDIUM 2-5 A '000	B % DOWN	C % ACROSS	D INDEX	LIGHT LESS THAN 2 A '000	B % DOWN	C % ACROSS	D INDEX
ALL ADULTS	170599	27191	100.0	15.9	100	5493	100.0	3.2	100	7401	100.0	4.3	100	14296	100.0	8.4	100
MEN	81025	13970	51.4	17.2	108	3504	63.8	4.3	134	4030	54.5	5.0	115	6435	45.0	7.9	95
WOMEN	89573	13221	48.6	14.8	93	1989	36.2	2.2	69	3371	45.5	3.8	87	7861	55.0	8.8	105
HOUSEHOLD HEADS	93008	14789	54.4	15.9	100	3546	64.6	3.8	118	4448	60.6	4.8	111	6755	47.3	7.3	87
HOMEMAKERS	93183	13744	50.5	14.7	93	2386	43.4	2.6	80	3709	50.1	4.0	92	7648	53.5	8.2	98
GRADUATED COLLEGE	28587	7167	26.4	25.1	157	1082	19.7	3.8	117	2001	27.0	7.0	161	4085	28.6	14.3	171
ATTENDED COLLEGE	29580	5810	21.4	19.6	123	1206	22.0	4.1	127	1461	19.7	4.9	114	3144	22.0	10.6	127
GRADUATED HIGH SCHOOL	66991	10056	37.0	15.0	94	2094	38.1	3.1	97	2909	39.3	4.3	100	5053	35.3	7.5	90
DID NOT GRADUATE HIGH SCHOOL	45441	4157	15.3	9.1	57	1111	20.2	2.4	76	1030	13.9	2.3	52	2016	14.1	4.4	53
18-24	27990	6125	22.5	21.9	137	1341	24.4	4.8	149	1415	19.1	5.1	117	3369	23.6	12.0	144
25-34	40798	8993	33.1	22.0	138	1745	31.8	4.3	133	2253	30.4	5.5	127	4994	34.9	12.2	146
35-44	30486	5355	19.7	17.6	110	1077	19.6	3.5	110	1555	21.0	5.1	118	2723	19.0	8.9	107
45-54	22494	3150	11.6	14.0	88	547	10.0	2.4	75	1003	13.6	4.5	103	1601	11.2	7.1	85
55-64	22366	2208	8.1	9.9	62	517	9.4	2.3	72	668	9.0	3.0	69	1024	7.2	4.6	55
65 OR OVER	26465	1358	5.0	5.1	32	*265	4.8	1.0	31	507	6.9	1.9	44	586	4.1	2.2	26
18-34	68788	15119	55.6	22.0	138	3087	56.2	4.5	139	3668	49.6	5.3	123	8363	58.5	12.2	145
18-49	110764	22250	81.8	20.1	126	4469	81.4	4.0	125	5768	77.9	5.2	120	12012	84.0	10.8	129
25-54	93777	17499	64.4	18.7	117	3369	61.3	3.6	111	4811	65.0	5.1	118	9319	65.2	9.9	119
EMPLOYED FULL TIME	94634	18708	68.8	19.8	124	4071	74.1	4.3	134	5161	69.7	5.5	126	9476	66.3	10.0	119
PART-TIME	10214	2147	7.9	21.0	132	*438	8.0	4.3	133	*415	5.6	4.1	94	1293	9.0	12.7	151
NOT EMPLOYED	65750	6336	23.3	9.6	60	984	17.9	1.5	47	1825	24.7	2.8	64	3528	24.7	5.4	64
PROFESSIONAL	14039	3377	12.4	24.1	151	638	11.6	4.5	141	865	11.7	6.2	142	1874	13.1	13.3	159
EXECUTIVE/ADMIN./MANAGERIAL	12160	2892	10.6	23.8	149	592	10.8	4.9	151	887	12.0	7.3	168	1413	9.9	11.6	139
CLERICAL/SALES/TECHNICAL	32724	6496	23.9	19.9	125	1261	23.0	3.9	120	1679	22.7	5.1	118	3555	24.9	10.9	130
PRECISION, CRAFTS, REPAIR	13286	2221	8.2	16.7	105	576	10.5	4.3	135	654	8.8	4.9	113	990	6.9	7.5	89
OTHER EMPLOYED	32640	5870	21.6	18.0	113	1441	26.2	4.4	137	1492	20.2	4.6	105	2937	20.5	9.0	107
H/D INCOME $50,000 OR MORE	31512	6843	25.2	21.7	136	1235	22.5	3.9	122	1851	25.0	5.9	135	3757	26.3	11.9	142
$40,000 - 49,999	23129	4504	16.6	19.5	122	820	14.9	3.5	110	1361	18.4	5.9	135	2323	16.3	10.0	120
$35,000 - 39,999	14364	2780	10.2	19.4	121	423	7.7	2.9	91	837	11.3	5.8	134	1518	10.6	10.6	126
$25,000 - 34,999	32979	5397	19.8	16.4	103	1146	20.9	3.5	108	1335	18.0	4.0	93	2915	20.4	8.8	105
$15,000 - 24,999	33695	4470	16.4	13.3	83	1009	18.4	3.0	93	1250	16.9	3.7	85	2212	15.5	6.6	78
LESS THAN $15,000	34919	3198	11.8	9.2	57	859	15.6	2.5	76	767	10.4	2.2	51	1571	11.0	4.5	54
CENSUS REGION: NORTH EAST	36650	5549	20.4	15.1	95	911	16.6	2.5	77	1213	16.4	3.3	76	3424	24.0	9.3	111
NORTH CENTRAL	42338	8207	30.2	19.4	122	1717	31.3	4.1	126	2456	33.2	5.8	134	4034	28.2	9.5	114
SOUTH	58325	7907	29.1	13.6	85	1909	34.8	3.3	102	2337	31.6	4.0	92	3661	25.6	6.3	75
WEST	33286	5529	20.3	16.6	104	956	17.4	2.9	89	1396	18.9	4.2	97	3178	22.2	9.5	114
MARKETING REG.: NEW ENGLAND	9345	1797	6.6	19.2	121	*349	6.4	3.7	116	418	5.6	4.5	103	1030	7.2	11.0	132
MIDDLE ATLANTIC	30750	4407	16.2	14.3	90	738	13.4	2.4	75	955	12.9	3.1	72	2714	19.0	8.8	105
EAST CENTRAL	23810	4064	14.9	17.1	107	791	14.4	3.3	103	1138	15.4	4.8	110	2134	14.9	9.0	107
WEST CENTRAL	27882	5364	19.7	19.2	121	1065	19.4	3.8	119	1563	21.1	5.6	129	2735	19.1	9.8	117
SOUTH EAST	30767	3880	14.3	12.6	79	916	16.7	3.0	93	1217	16.4	4.0	91	1746	12.2	5.7	68
SOUTH WEST	19241	2928	10.8	15.2	95	771	14.0	4.0	125	852	11.5	4.4	102	1306	9.1	6.8	81
PACIFIC	28804	4753	17.5	16.5	104	861	15.7	3.0	93	1260	17.0	4.4	101	2632	18.4	9.1	109

COUNTY SIZE A	70655	11724	43.1	16.6	104	2184	39.8	3.1	96	3213	43.4	4.5	105	6327	44.3	9.0	107
COUNTY SIZE B	50905	8752	32.2	17.2	108	1801	32.8	3.5	110	2495	33.7	4.9	113	4457	31.2	8.8	105
COUNTY SIZE C	25845	3599	13.2	13.9	87	962	17.5	3.7	116	821	11.1	3.2	73	1816	12.7	7.0	84
COUNTY SIZE D	23194	3116	11.5	13.4	84	546	9.9	2.4	73	874	11.8	3.8	87	1697	11.9	7.3	87
MSA CENTRAL CITY	60762	10225	37.6	16.8	106	2193	39.9	3.6	112	2945	39.8	4.8	112	5087	35.6	8.4	100
MSA SUBURBAN	69857	11650	42.8	16.7	105	2167	39.5	3.1	96	3082	41.6	4.4	102	6400	44.8	9.2	109
NON-MSA	39979	5316	19.6	13.3	83	1133	20.6	2.8	88	1374	18.6	3.4	79	2810	19.7	7.0	84
SINGLE	35891	7628	28.1	21.3	133	1777	32.4	5.0	154	1827	24.7	5.1	117	4023	28.1	11.2	134
MARRIED	104358	15905	58.5	15.2	96	2762	50.3	2.6	82	4408	59.6	4.2	97	8735	61.1	8.4	100
OTHER	30350	3659	13.5	12.1	76	954	17.4	3.1	98	1167	15.8	3.8	89	1539	10.8	5.1	61
PARENTS	58376	10389	38.2	17.8	112	1840	33.5	3.2	98	2757	37.3	4.7	109	5793	40.5	9.9	118
WORKING PARENTS	42642	8191	30.1	19.2	121	1566	28.5	3.7	114	2189	29.6	5.1	118	4436	31.0	10.4	124
HOUSEHOLD SIZE: 1 PERSON	20017	2400	8.8	12.0	75	682	12.4	3.4	106	574	7.8	2.9	66	1145	8.0	5.7	68
2 PERSONS	51418	7632	28.1	14.8	93	1472	26.8	2.9	89	2354	31.8	4.6	106	3807	26.6	7.4	88
3 OR MORE	99163	17159	63.1	17.3	109	3340	60.8	3.4	105	4474	60.5	4.5	104	9346	65.4	9.4	112
ANY CHILD IN HOUSEHOLD	70885	12252	45.1	17.3	108	2244	40.9	3.2	98	3246	43.9	4.6	106	6764	47.3	9.5	114
UNDER 2 YEARS	13195	2398	8.8	18.2	114	*259	4.7	2.0	61	645	8.7	4.9	113	1493	10.4	11.3	135
2-5 YEARS	25191	4423	16.3	17.6	110	759	13.8	3.0	93	1051	14.2	4.2	96	2613	18.3	10.4	124
6-11 YEARS	29786	4972	18.3	16.7	105	991	18.0	3.3	103	1275	17.2	4.3	99	2707	18.9	9.1	108
12-17 YEARS	35106	5808	21.4	16.5	104	1183	21.5	3.4	105	1472	19.9	4.2	97	3153	22.1	9.0	107
WHITE	148266	24915	91.6	16.8	105	5046	91.9	3.4	106	6677	90.2	4.5	104	13192	92.3	8.9	106
BLACK	18639	1766	6.5	9.5	59	*370	6.7	2.0	62	557	7.5	3.0	69	839	5.9	4.5	54
HOME OWNED	119945	18365	67.5	15.3	96	3427	62.4	2.9	89	5062	68.4	4.2	97	9876	69.1	8.2	98
TELEVISION:EARLY NEWS	86378	11694	43.0	13.5	85	2327	42.4	2.7	84	3686	49.8	4.3	98	5681	39.7	6.6	79
LATE NEWS	70899	10770	39.6	15.2	95	1909	34.8	2.7	84	3034	41.0	4.3	99	5827	40.8	8.2	98
DAILY NEWSPAPERS: READ ANY	103229	16897	62.1	16.4	103	3296	60.0	3.2	99	4697	63.5	4.6	105	8904	62.3	8.6	103
READ ONE DAILY	77451	12284	45.2	15.9	99	2396	43.6	3.1	96	3386	45.8	4.4	101	6501	45.5	8.4	100
READ TWO OR MORE DAILIES	25778	4614	17.0	17.9	112	900	16.4	3.5	108	1311	17.7	5.1	117	2404	16.8	9.3	111
SUNDAY NEWSPAPERS: READ ANY	111867	18744	68.9	16.8	105	3639	66.2	3.3	101	5300	71.6	4.7	109	9805	68.6	8.8	105
READ ONE SUNDAY	95256	15468	56.9	16.2	102	2940	53.5	3.1	96	4437	60.0	4.7	107	8091	56.6	8.5	101
READ TWO OR MORE SUNDAYS	16611	3276	12.0	19.7	124	700	12.7	4.2	131	862	11.6	5.2	120	1714	12.0	10.3	123
HEAVY MAGAZINES - HEAVY TV	42778	6942	25.5	16.2	102	1570	28.6	3.7	114	1977	26.7	4.6	106	3396	23.8	7.9	95
HEAVY MAGAZINES - LIGHT TV	42528	9269	34.1	21.8	137	1848	33.6	4.3	135	2348	31.7	5.5	127	5074	35.5	11.9	142
LIGHT MAGAZINES - HEAVY TV	42512	4950	18.2	11.6	73	999	18.2	2.3	73	1449	19.6	3.4	79	2503	17.5	5.9	70
LIGHT MAGAZINES - LIGHT TV	42781	6030	22.2	14.1	88	1078	19.6	2.5	78	1628	22.0	3.8	88	3325	23.3	7.8	93
QUINTILE I - OUTDOOR	34087	6886	25.3	20.2	127	1399	25.5	4.1	127	2124	28.7	6.2	144	3363	23.5	9.9	118
QUINTILE II	34137	6297	23.2	18.4	116	1293	23.5	3.8	118	1833	24.8	5.4	124	3172	22.2	9.3	111
QUINTILE III	34126	5196	19.1	15.2	96	878	16.0	2.6	80	1293	17.5	3.8	87	3024	21.2	8.9	106
QUINTILE IV	34112	4659	17.1	13.7	86	868	15.8	2.5	79	1088	14.7	3.2	74	2703	18.9	7.9	95
QUINTILE V	34137	4152	15.3	12.2	76	1055	19.2	3.1	96	1063	14.4	3.1	72	2034	14.2	6.0	71
QUINTILE I - MAGAZINES	34124	7108	26.1	20.8	131	1376	25.1	4.0	125	1605	21.7	4.7	108	4127	28.9	12.1	144
QUINTILE II	34114	6321	23.2	18.5	116	1284	23.4	3.8	117	1972	26.6	5.8	133	3066	21.4	9.0	107
QUINTILE III	34110	5241	19.3	15.4	96	1179	21.5	3.5	107	1533	20.7	4.5	103	2528	17.7	7.4	88
QUINTILE IV	34121	4743	17.4	13.9	87	942	17.1	2.8	86	1360	18.4	4.0	92	2440	17.1	7.2	85
QUINTILE V	34129	3777	13.9	11.1	69	713	13.0	2.1	65	931	12.6	2.7	63	2135	14.9	6.3	75

Spring 1986

Source: Mediamark Research Inc., Spring 1986

Figure 3.7

LOW CALORIE DOMESTIC BEER 123

BASE: ADULTS	TOTAL U.S. '000	BUDWEISER LIGHT A '000	B % DOWN	C % ACROSS	D INDEX	COORS LIGHT A '000	B % DOWN	C % ACROSS	D INDEX	MICHELOB LIGHT A '000	B % DOWN	C % ACROSS	D INDEX	MILLER LITE A '000	B % DOWN	C % ACROSS	D INDEX
ALL ADULTS	170599	7819	100.0	4.6	100	6297	100.0	3.7	100	4982	100.0	2.9	100	13404	100.0	7.9	100
MEN	81025	4617	59.0	5.7	124	3148	50.0	3.9	105	2378	47.7	2.9	100	6987	52.1	8.6	110
WOMEN	89573	3203	41.0	3.6	78	3149	50.0	3.5	95	2604	52.3	2.9	100	6417	47.9	7.2	91
HOUSEHOLD HEADS	93008	4328	55.4	4.7	102	3354	53.3	3.6	98	2833	56.9	3.0	104	7470	55.7	8.0	102
HOMEMAKERS	93183	3447	44.1	3.7	81	3118	49.5	3.3	91	2554	51.3	2.7	94	6827	50.9	7.3	93
GRADUATED COLLEGE	28587	2158	27.6	7.5	165	1617	25.7	5.7	153	1492	29.9	5.2	179	3909	29.2	13.7	174
ATTENDED COLLEGE	29580	1685	21.6	5.7	124	1845	29.3	6.2	169	1345	27.0	4.5	156	2835	21.2	9.6	122
GRADUATED HIGH SCHOOL	66991	2909	37.2	4.3	95	2007	31.9	3.0	81	1474	29.6	2.2	75	4840	36.1	7.2	92
DID NOT GRADUATE HIGH SCHOOL	45441	1067	13.6	2.3	51	828	13.1	1.8	49	670	13.4	1.5	50	1820	13.6	4.0	51
18-24	27990	2444	31.3	8.7	191	1634	25.9	5.8	158	1276	25.6	4.6	156	2908	21.7	10.4	132
25-34	40798	2318	29.6	5.7	124	1990	31.6	4.9	132	1945	39.0	4.8	163	4923	36.7	12.1	154
35-44	30486	1481	18.9	4.9	106	1231	19.5	4.0	109	741	14.9	2.4	83	2467	18.4	8.1	103
45-54	22494	876	11.2	3.9	85	706	11.2	3.1	85	456	9.2	2.0	70	1440	10.7	6.4	81
55-64	22366	419	5.4	1.9	41	475	7.5	2.1	57	*431	8.7	1.9	66	1147	8.6	5.1	65
65 OR OVER	26465	*282	3.6	1.1	23	*261	4.1	1.0	27	*132	2.6	.5	17	519	3.9	2.0	25
18-34	68788	4762	60.9	6.9	151	3624	57.6	5.3	143	3221	64.7	4.7	160	7831	58.4	11.4	145
18-49	110764	6746	86.3	6.1	133	5339	84.8	4.8	131	4216	84.6	3.8	130	11145	83.1	10.1	128
25-54	93777	4674	59.8	5.0	109	3927	62.4	4.2	114	3142	63.1	3.4	115	8830	65.9	9.4	120
EMPLOYED FULL TIME	94634	5541	70.9	5.9	128	4279	68.0	4.5	122	3610	72.5	3.8	130	9584	71.5	10.1	129
PART-TIME	10214	586	7.5	5.7	125	*375	6.0	3.7	99	*484	9.7	4.7	162	1014	7.6	9.9	126
NOT EMPLOYED	65750	1692	21.6	2.6	56	1643	26.1	2.5	68	887	17.8	1.3	46	2807	20.9	4.3	54
PROFESSIONAL	14039	961	12.3	6.8	150	708	11.2	5.0	137	843	16.9	6.0	205	2019	15.1	14.4	183
EXECUTIVE/ADMIN/MANAGERIAL	12160	832	10.6	6.8	149	778	12.4	6.4	173	563	11.3	4.6	159	1293	9.6	10.6	135
CLERICAL/SALES/TECHNICAL	32724	1701	21.8	5.2	114	1718	27.3	5.2	142	1249	25.1	3.8	131	3408	25.4	10.4	132
PRECISION, CRAFTS, REPAIR	13286	768	9.8	5.8	126	*382	6.1	2.9	78	546	11.0	4.1	141	1124	8.4	8.5	108
OTHER EMPLOYED	32640	1865	23.9	5.7	125	1068	17.0	3.3	89	893	17.9	2.7	94	2754	20.5	8.4	107
H/D INCOME $50,000 OR MORE	31512	2018	25.8	6.4	140	1892	30.0	6.0	163	1286	25.8	4.1	140	3527	26.3	11.2	142
$40,000 - 49,999	23129	1204	15.4	5.2	114	877	13.9	3.8	103	907	18.2	3.9	134	2522	18.8	10.9	139
$35,000 - 39,999	14364	813	10.4	5.7	124	517	8.2	3.6	98	465	9.3	3.2	111	1476	11.0	10.3	131
$25,000 - 34,999	32979	1600	20.5	4.9	106	1259	20.0	3.8	104	1005	20.2	3.0	104	2328	17.4	7.1	90
$15,000 - 24,999	33695	1225	15.7	3.6	79	1179	18.7	3.5	95	780	15.7	2.3	79	2197	16.4	6.5	83
LESS THAN $15,000	34919	961	12.3	2.8	60	573	9.1	1.6	44	538	10.8	1.5	53	1353	10.1	3.9	49
CENSUS REGION: NORTH EAST	36650	1597	20.4	4.4	95	649	10.3	1.8	48	1367	27.4	3.7	128	2496	18.6	6.8	87
NORTH CENTRAL	42338	2146	27.4	5.1	111	1429	22.7	3.4	92	1278	25.7	3.0	103	4603	34.3	10.8	138
SOUTH	58325	1814	23.2	3.1	68	2440	38.7	4.2	113	1329	26.7	2.3	78	3978	29.7	6.8	131
WEST	33286	2262	28.9	6.8	148	1779	28.3	5.3	145	1007	20.2	3.0	104	2327	17.4	7.0	89

	Total '000	'000	%	%	Index	'000	%	%	Index	'000	%	%	Index	'000	%	%	Index
MARKETING REG.: NEW ENGLAND	9345	517	6.6	5.5	121	449	7.1	4.8	130	542	10.9	5.8	199	869	6.5	9.3	118
MIDDLE ATLANTIC	30750	1228	15.7	4.0	87	*325	5.2	1.1	29	904	18.1	2.9	101	2014	15.0	6.5	83
EAST CENTRAL	23810	997	12.8	4.2	91	523	8.3	2.2	60	834	16.7	3.5	120	2252	16.8	9.5	120
WEST CENTRAL	27882	1555	19.9	5.6	122	1315	20.9	4.7	128	568	11.4	2.0	70	2986	22.3	10.7	136
SOUTH EAST	30767	925	11.8	3.0	66	1171	18.6	3.8	103	875	17.6	2.8	97	2095	15.6	6.8	87
SOUTH WEST	19241	601	7.7	3.1	68	1089	17.3	5.7	153	*327	6.6	1.7	58	1323	9.9	6.9	88
PACIFIC	28804	1997	25.5	6.9	151	1425	22.6	4.9	134	932	18.7	3.2	111	1865	13.9	6.5	82
COUNTY SIZE A	70655	3056	39.1	4.3	95	2714	43.1	3.8	104	2455	49.3	3.5	119	6125	45.7	8.7	110
COUNTY SIZE B	50905	2548	32.6	5.0	109	2014	32.0	4.0	107	1632	32.8	3.2	110	4384	32.7	8.6	110
COUNTY SIZE C	25845	907	11.6	3.5	77	796	12.6	3.1	83	641	12.9	2.5	85	1767	13.2	6.8	87
COUNTY SIZE D	23194	1308	16.7	5.6	123	773	12.3	3.3	90	*253	5.1	1.1	37	1129	8.4	4.9	62
MSA CENTRAL CITY	60762	2639	33.8	4.3	95	2397	38.1	3.9	107	2052	41.2	3.4	116	5496	41.0	9.0	115
MSA SUBURBAN	69857	3318	42.4	4.7	104	2482	39.4	3.6	96	2231	44.8	3.2	109	5737	42.8	8.2	115
NON-MSA	39979	1862	23.8	4.7	102	1419	22.5	3.5	96	698	14.0	1.7	60	2171	16.2	5.4	69
SINGLE	35891	2797	35.8	7.8	170	1759	27.9	4.9	133	1633	32.8	4.5	156	3827	28.6	10.7	136
MARRIED	104358	4044	51.7	3.9	85	3827	60.8	3.7	99	2796	56.1	2.7	92	7842	58.5	7.5	96
OTHER	30350	978	12.5	3.2	70	710	11.3	2.3	63	553	11.1	1.8	62	1736	13.0	5.7	73
PARENTS	58376	2922	37.4	5.0	109	2405	38.2	4.1	112	1852	37.2	3.2	109	4993	37.3	8.6	109
WORKING PARENTS	42642	2353	30.1	5.5	121	1827	29.0	4.3	116	1454	29.2	3.4	117	3992	29.8	9.4	119
HOUSEHOLD SIZE: 1 PERSON	20017	727	9.3	3.6	79	526	8.4	2.6	71	515	10.3	2.6	88	1336	10.0	6.7	85
2 PERSONS	51418	2259	28.9	4.4	96	1818	28.9	3.5	96	1438	28.9	2.8	96	3884	29.0	7.6	96
3 OR MORE	99163	4833	61.8	4.9	106	3952	62.8	4.0	108	3028	60.8	3.1	104	8184	61.1	8.3	105
ANY CHILD IN HOUSEHOLD	70885	3573	45.7	5.0	110	2889	45.9	4.1	111	2229	44.7	3.1	108	5718	42.7	8.1	103
UNDER 2 YEARS	13195	658	8.4	5.0	109	607	9.6	4.6	125	431	8.7	3.3	112	1193	8.9	9.0	115
2-5 YEARS	25191	1272	16.3	5.0	110	1058	16.8	4.2	114	924	18.5	3.7	126	2234	16.7	8.9	113
6-11 YEARS	29786	1474	18.9	4.9	108	1146	18.2	3.8	104	924	18.5	3.1	106	2439	18.2	8.2	104
12-17 YEARS	35106	1849	23.6	5.3	115	1382	21.9	3.9	107	846	17.0	2.4	83	2608	19.5	7.4	95
WHITE	148266	7039	90.0	4.7	104	5880	93.4	4.0	108	4663	93.6	3.1	108	12172	90.8	8.2	104
BLACK	18639	622	8.0	3.3	73	*280	4.4	1.5	41	*151	3.0	.8	28	938	7.0	5.0	64
HOME OWNED	119945	4806	61.5	4.0	88	4353	69.1	3.6	98	3126	62.7	2.6	89	8811	65.7	7.3	94

Spring 1986

Source: Mediamark Research Inc., Spring 1986

Precautions. It is important to remember some basic precautions that should be exercised in interpreting and applying syndicated research reports. Although it may appear obvious that the media planner should have a thorough understanding of exactly what he or she is using as decision-making inputs, the simplest prerequisite (sometimes overlooked!) to utilize syndicated research properly is to *read the instructions* provided by the research organization. SMRB and MRI, for example, have between them some fundamental differences in technique that require a basic understanding by the planner if the reported information is to be properly applied. Further recognize that media research reports are based on samples that vary in size and methodology.

Another precaution concerns the simple misuse of numbers or the failure to comprehend the interrelationships between numbers. For example, while indices provided by syndicated reports are useful for establishing common denominators, an index must be related to the percent of the user base that is represented before any meaningful conclusions can be drawn.

Limitations. In order to use SMRB and MRI data intelligently, you must also understand their limitations. These services do not define markets for you. Although the data do describe demographically the users of products and brands, the decision rests with marketing planners as to which market segments represent the greatest sales potential. Only after the targeting decision has been made will syndicated research reports assist the media planner in seeking out these segments via the most appropriate media vehicles. Moreover, remember that the data contained in such reports are static, rather than dynamic, pictures of the marketplace that describe consumption patterns at a fixed point in time. The greatest danger in attempting to let syndicated services define markets for you lies in the erroneous assumption that there are no changes occurring in market structure or consumption habits. In fact, syndicated research reports are history and targeting decisions based solely on data from these reports bear the burden of following the marketplace. Reported information on any product may simply be an obituary of mistakes made by that product's marketers.

In summary, then, use SMRB, MRI, and other services as inputs to media selection decisions and not as a means of deciding to whom products should be marketed.

The Final Linkage Between Target Markets and Vehicle Audiences

Thus far we have talked about the parameters for defining target markets as well as the ways in which media vehicle audiences are described. Now we must concern ourselves with the alternative methods of applying these audience descriptions to consummate the media-market match. The alternatives to be described are diagrammatically summarized in Figure 3.8.

The simplest situation for matching exists when the target market has been defined in terms of demographic characteristics. The media planner may directly seek demographic profiles of media vehicle audiences and select those vehicles whose audiences most closely approximate the target market description.

When the target market has been defined in terms of product usage, however, two options for effecting the match are available to the media planner. The first alternative and the most direct approach is to seek data that shows to which media vehicles the heavy, medium, light, or non-users are exposed. If, for example, the target market is the heavy user, the media planner can directly identify the vehicles to which heavy users of the product are exposed. This approach eliminates the media planner's need for comprehensive demographic data since product usage is the common denominator in the target market and vehicle audience descriptions.

For matching vehicle audiences to target markets defined in terms of product usage, a second alternative involves a two-step process of seeking matchable information. The first step is to seek the demographic profiles of media vehicle audiences. The second step is to seek demographic profiles of heavy, medium, light, or non-users of the product. The audience profiles are then matched to the profiles of product users. This less direct approach may be desirable if: (1) information on product users' media exposure is not available, (2) creative strategy relies heavily on a knowledge of the target market's demographic characteristics, (3) demographics significantly influence other marketing elements, such as distribution, or (4) frequency of use is unknown as in the introduction of a new product, in which case the planner would focus on total usage in the product category as a basis for media-market matching.

Figure 3.8

Alternative Approaches to the Media-Market Matching Process

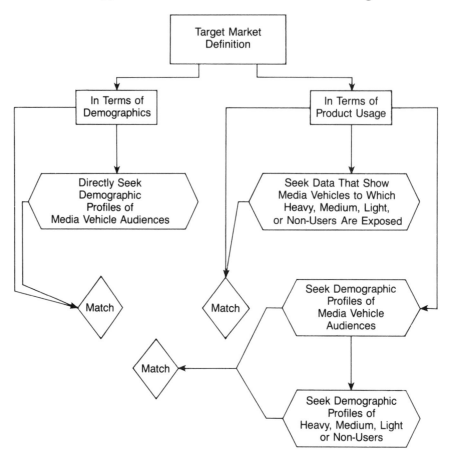

More Than One Target Market: A Question of Relative Emphasis

In the midst of many references in this chapter to "the target market," let it be clearly understood that marketers do not necessarily confine their efforts to one target. Target markets are often broken down into a primary market, a secondary market, and so on, with each receiving a certain degree of advertising emphasis.

We may illustrate such a breakdown with a situation in which the product's end user and purchasing agent are not one and the same. Consider, for example, that the end user of a children's toy will be a child, but the purchasing agent will be a parent. The marketer must determine the relative value of each of these markets (children and parents) in terms of their influence on the purchasing decision. If research shows that the child has highly significant influence on the parent's decision to purchase this particular product, the marketer may designate children as the primary market and parents as the secondary market. This indicates that more marketing communication emphasis will be placed on children than on parents.

The decision regarding relative emphasis is largely a subjective one, but it has direct effects on media selection decisions. Suppose that in the foregoing example the primary and secondary markets were weighted 70%/30%. Seventy percent of the media effort might be channeled into Saturday morning television in order to reach the child, with 30 percent in general editorial magazines in order to reach the child's parents.

Summary

This chapter has introduced the focal point of the marketing plan— the target market. After noting that all marketing efforts are aimed at these target consumers, we discussed the importance of matching media vehicle audiences and target market descriptions. This media-market match is the means by which media vehicles are ultimately selected after relative costs and creative requirements have been considered. The quality of media decisions at the tactical level is therefore heavily dependent on the precision of media-market matches.

Parameters for defining target markets were also discussed, including demographic characteristics, sociopsychological variables, and product/brand usage. The various types of target market definitions can be applied to media decisions in different ways and alternative approaches to media-market matching were explained and illustrated via flowchart.

Syndicated research services, including SMRB and MRI, were reviewed in the context of how these tools can help media planners in the matching process.

Finally, the concept of primary versus secondary target markets was introduced, highlighting the decision regarding the degree of *relative* emphasis that should be placed on each target.

Endnotes

1. David L. Kurtz and Louis E. Boone, *Marketing,* 2nd edition (Hinsdale, Ill.: Dryden Press, 1984), p. 87; for a full discussion of market segmentation, see pages 85-130 of this text.

2. For a description of the nine sub-categories, see S. Watson Dunn and Arnold M. Barban, *Advertising: Its Role in Modern Marketing,* 6th edition (Hinsdale, Ill.: Dryden Press, 1986), pp. 303-304.

3. Leo Bogart, *Strategy in Advertising,* 2nd edition (Lincolnwood: Crain Books/ NTC Business Books, 1984), p. 251.

4. Jack Z. Sissors and Jim Surmanek, *Advertising Media Planning,* 2nd edition (Lincolnwood: Crain Books/NTC Business Books, 1982), p. 122.

Chapter Four

Media Objectives

A Perspective on Media Objectives

Establishing media objectives is the first step in the actual process of formulating the media plan. We could not, however, establish these objectives without knowledge of the subject matter in the three preceding chapters. In viewing media objectives in the context of the total marketing picture, we see that these goals must flow from marketing and advertising plans as discussed in Chapter 2 and must be geared to pinpointed target markets as discussed in Chapter 3.

Before exploring the nature of media objectives and general guidelines for establishing them, it is necessary to develop an understanding of some key concepts upon which media objectives are built.

Concepts Essential to the Establishment of Media Objectives

Concepts which are indispensable to the media planner in formulating objectives include: (1) reach, (2) frequency, and (3) continuity. Directly related to reach and frequency is the gross rating point; although more significant in the tactics of media buying than at the strategic level of planning, the gross rating point is an important part of the media planner's lexicon and will also be explained in this section.

Reach and Frequency

Reach may be defined as the unduplicated proportion of a population that is exposed to the advertising message at least once during a designated time period (usually four weeks). *Frequency* refers to the number of times within the four-week period that a prospect or a portion of the population is exposed to the message.

Frequency may be expressed in two ways: as a straight average or as a distribution (hence the term, *frequency distribution*). If frequency is stated as an average of 3.0, for example, the average prospect is exposed to the message three times during the four-week period. But certainly all prospects are not exposed exactly three times; rather, some are exposed more than three times and some less, producing a distribution of frequency levels that average to 3.0.

For example, the following frequency distribution has 3.0 as its average, but you can readily see the number of people who were exposed to more than three and less than three messages:

Number of Exposures in Four-Week Period	Number of People Exposed
1	25
2	20
3	45
4	25
5	15
6	5
	135

Frequency distribution does not necessarily figure heavily in the formulation of frequency objectives. In stating goals, the media planner is likely to express the average frequency that he or she is willing to accept. The frequency distribution serves as a post hoc measure of the variability of that average. Suppose, for example, that your target market consists of women between the ages of 25 and 49. Your frequency distribution may show that you have attained a high frequency level among older women (ages 35-49) and a low frequency level among younger women (ages 25-34). Frequency expressed as a straight average does not offer this information which is of significant value to the media planner in assessing the impact of the media schedule.

It is important to note that frequency objectives are a very difficult decision area because the importance of frequency depends upon the effects of repetition, which we still know relatively little about.[1]

Continuity

Continuity refers to how advertising is scheduled over the time span of a campaign period. (The term "continuity" is, unfortunately, a classic example of the ambiguity of media terminology. While some media practitioners define this term as continuous advertising over a specified time period, the existing body of media literature more often uses the term to refer to the overall consideration of timing in media scheduling. This latter context is the one in which the term continuity is used in this chapter—to encompass the entire dimension of timing, that is, whether media are scheduled continuously or in separated periods of media usage.) On one extreme of the time dimension is continuous advertising in which the media effort remains relatively constant on an ongoing basis throughout the entire campaign period.

The strategies of *flighting* and *pulsing* are in contrast to a continuous effort. Under a flighting pattern, media effort is varied over the campaign period, with some periods of time receiving *no* advertising. The pulsing strategy has noted variation in media use over time, but exerts at least some media effort during every period of the campaign. Figure 4.1 graphically shows the three types of continuity.

A typical pattern for many advertisers is to exert a heavy media effort just prior to traditional peaks in the sales curve and to maintain a light media effort at all other times during the campaign period (for example, pulsing). This situation is demonstrated in the following example. Suppose you are preparing a 12-month media schedule for the manufacturer of a well-known brand of quality boxed confections. Since it is a popular gift item, the demand for this type of candy traditionally peaks just before St. Valentine's Day, Mother's Day, and Christmas. Accordingly, you may want to schedule an intense media effort in early February, early and mid-May, and December, while delivering a low level of advertising (or no advertising at all) during the remainder of the campaign period.

Occasionally, marketers try the converse; that is, scheduling the media effort inversely to the sales curve. The intended result is to smooth out the sales curve in order to reap the cost-cutting advantages of stabilized production of the product throughout the year. Application of flighting/pulsing in a way that parallels the expected sales, however, is the approach that is far more often practiced.

Figure 4.1

Three Patterns of Media Continuity

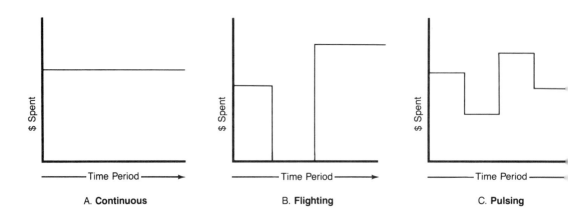

A. **Continuous**   B. **Flighting**   C. **Pulsing**

Regardless of the media continuity pattern used, remember that the decision to employ a particular strategy is largely determined by the expected relative volume of business during intervals within the campaign period. That volume is usually expressed as a projected sales curve with which the media planner should always be armed.

The Gross Rating Point

Gross rating point is a term that has become an essential part of the media decision maker's vocabulary. The gross rating point (GRP) is used to characterize the gross weight of a given media effort against a defined target market. That effort may be anything from a single media buy to a combination of many media buys over the time span of an entire campaign period. Quantitatively speaking, gross rating points equal reach multiplied by average frequency (GRP = R × F) GRPs therefore describe the gross weight of advertising that is being absorbed by the market during a designated period in the media schedule. For example, if we bought media that reached 70 percent of our designated target, with an average frequency of 3.0 exposures, we could describe this effort as having delivered 210 GRPs ($70 \times 3.0 = 210$).

Let's summarize our discussion to date by providing a sample situation to exemplify the concepts. The table below shows how a community of 10 television homes (A through J) watched Program X over a four-week period:

Week	A	B	C	D	E	F	G	H	I	J	Total Exposures
1	X							X			2
2		X		X	X			X			4
3	X						X	X			3
4					X			X		X	3
Total Exposures	2	1	0	1	2	0	1	4	0	1	12

We see that seven of the ten homes watched Program X at least once during the four-week period (Homes C, F, and I did not watch). Thus, our reach was 7 homes, or 70 percent (7 of 10 = 70%). The frequency distribution is:

Number of Exposures in 4-week Period	Number of Homes Exposed
0	3 (Homes C, F, I)
1	4 (Homes B, D, G, J)
2	2 (Homes A, E)
3	0
4	1 (Home H)

The "average" of such a distribution is 1.71

$$\frac{(1 \times 4) + (2 \times 2) + (4 \times 1)}{7} = \frac{12}{7} = 1.71$$

Thus, we can say that our average frequency is 1.71 exposures. And, since GRP = Reach X Average Frequency, this example produced 120 GRPs (70 × 1.71 = 119.7 = 120).

The Reach-Frequency Trade-Off

Can the planner set media objectives calling for maximization of both reach and frequency? Not realistically, for in the intention to fulfill such goals lies a most fundamental oversight. The relationship between reach and frequency is such that only a magical budget of unlimited dollars could allow maximum emphasis on each in the same media schedule.

An analogy might be helpful here. You may recall the phenomenon of the unattainable triad[2] with respect to print production. The triad consists of quality of reproduction, speed of reproduction, and cost savings. Maximizing all three of these areas for the same job is an unattainable objective, because increasing quality means a sacrifice of money and speed, increasing savings means a sacrifice of quality and speed, and increasing speed usually requires a sacrifice of money and quality.

The reach-frequency relationship is very much the same. In light of the budget constraints within which media planners must always work, the direct trade-off between reach and frequency dictates that any move toward maximizing reach results in a sacrifice of frequency, and vice versa. Consider this in the perspective of the time dimension, and you will see that we have another unattainable triad, consisting of continuity as well as reach and frequency. If the advertiser is willing to take a periodic hiatus during the campaign period, the budget will allow both reach and frequency to be enhanced during each flight of advertising. Conversely, since a steady flow of media dollars is needed to support continuous advertising, a continuous schedule limits the opportunity to maximize reach or frequency during any portion of the campaign period.

General Guidelines for the Formulation of Media Objectives

There are several areas of consideration in which the media planner needs guidelines for purchasing advertising time and space. Such areas for goal establishment include: reach and frequency, continuity over time, competitive approach, merchandising support requirements, creative requirements of the message, and corporate policy considerations.

In the last three of these areas, the media objective is almost a given—that is, the media planner will always want to seek vehicles that offer substantial merchandising support, which meet the creative requirements of the message, and which have an image consistent with the corporate policies of the advertiser. But the areas of reach and frequency, continuity, and competitive approach lead us to structural objectives that differ tremendously from one marketing situation to the next. We are now ready to consider various ways to approach media objectives in these areas.

Structural Media Goals

Rules of thumb for formulating media objectives with respect to reach and frequency are indeed difficult to nail down. Because every media planning situation is different, no absolute guidelines exist for across-the-board application to reach and frequency decisions at the objective level. Thus, there are no pat answers to the questions of under what conditions reach is more important and under what conditions frequency is more important to the overall media strategy.

There are, however, some general guidelines that media planners find useful for establishing reach and frequency goals and for gaining insight into requirements for continuity and the competitive approach. One such guideline is the product life cycle, which was explained briefly in Chapter 2.

Product Life Cycle. The media planner's ability to use product life cycle as a meaningful guide to formulating objectives depends upon his understanding of the relationships between various life cycle stages and media strategy. Developing such an understanding for a particular product or brand is indeed difficult, so let us examine some of these relationships.

We said in Chapter 2 that creating awareness was important for a new product; thus, in the introductory stage of the product life cycle, it is probable that reach will be more important to the overall media strategy than will frequency. Establishing a handsome reach objective will give the media planner a springboard for developing a strategy to deliver the new product story to the largest possible percentage of the target market.

Media planners for brands in the introductory stage of the life cycle must pay extra special attention to the competitive approach outlined in the advertising strategy. Sometimes a new brand will be positioned head-on against the market leader; often, however, the new entry will seek to capture a small segment of the market that has been somewhat neglected by the market leader. In the latter case, the need for reach in product introduction is superseded by the need for a high–level of frequency against the small market segment.

In later stages of the product life cycle we find other implications for media objectives. As was also pointed out in Chapter 2, established products in the maturity stage of the life cycle often employ the technique of reminder advertising. The media planner can best contribute to the execution of such an advertising strategy by emphasizing, in the frequency objectives, the necessity of maximizing the number of messages delivered.

The stage in the product life cycle tends to be a significant influence on the level of promotional dollars that management is willing to invest during each advertising campaign period. This, therefore, is another way in which product life cycle affects reach, frequency, and continuity objectives—given that these objectives are always set within a budgetary framework. We typically find that proportionately more promotional dollars are available during the introductory stage in the life cycle, probably because many advertisers subscribe to the logic underlying what has come to be called "Peckham's Formula."[3]

The formula states that beginning with the initial product introduction and continuing for a two-year period, the advertiser should produce a share of advertising approximately equal to one and one-half times the share of sales being sought. Management's cognizance of the importance of outspending the competition in order to secure market share for a new product provides the media planner with the financial resources necessary to increase reach and frequency expectations in setting media objectives. This flow of promotional dollars has similar implications for the continuity of the media schedule.

There is yet another way in which the product life cycle may ultimately affect reach and frequency goals. Closely connected to the stage in the life cycle is the scope of the product's distribution system. It is quite conceivable, for example, that the number of distributors in the channel during the introductory stage may add up to only a fraction of the number that will stock the product in the latter part of the growth stage and in the maturity stage. The implication here is that a modest reach objective consistent with the scope of distribution might be in order, allowing a build-up in frequency. However, in a dynamic marketplace such as that of the grocery store, a marketer risks the loss of distribution if the introductory reach level does not generate sufficient movement off the shelf, relative to competition. If reach is built slowly, a low awareness level may result in such slow turnover that retailers currently stocking the brand may discontinue handling it. Since lost distribution, a manifestation of the retailer's lack of confidence in the brand, is difficult to regain, these factors should be weighed heavily in formulating reach objectives.

Breadth of Target Market. The extent, or breadth, of the target market is also an important determinant of structural media objectives. On one extreme, we have the target market that is widely dispersed geographically and demographically. Practical media objectives for delivering messages to such a market would call for pouring promotional dollars into reach and leaving frequency as a secondary concern.

On the other extreme, we have the target market that is narrowly defined, consisting of prospects that are largely homogeneous in terms of geography and demographic characteristics. Since it is less expensive to reach such a market segment, the thrust of the media effort may be higher frequency. Again the competitive approach comes to the fore since positioning strategy is a key determinant of the breadth of the target market.

Repurchase Cycle. Effective levels of reach and frequency and the desirability of continuous advertising also depend on the product's repurchase cycle. A soft drink may be purchased twice in the same day by the same customer, but it is likely to be years after the initial purchase of a major appliance or automobile that a repeat purchase will occur. If we abide by the theory that the best time to deliver an advertising message is when the prospect's propensity to consume is greatest, frequency requirements become more important for the product with a short repurchase cycle.

How are reach objectives influenced by repurchase cycles? Reach is particularly affected by very long repurchase cycles. A long cycle can breed market turnover to the extent that the target market's demographic characteristics may change.

What about the repurchase cycle's effect on continuity objectives? If a repurchase cycle can be isolated, the media planner may use that cycle as the key to discovering when flighting is an appropriate strategy. The media effort can be intensified just prior to expected repurchase, when the prospect's interest is high and his propensity to consume is at an optimal level.

Target Market Turnover. Related to the repurchase cycle is the idea that no matter how frequently the consumer repurchases a product, that product may only be useful for a short period of time in the consumer's life. Because this is true for products such as baby food, there is a great deal of target market turnover since purchasers of baby food will only use the product for one to two years regardless of how often they buy it. Thus, repurchase cycles should be considered in the broader context of target market turnover. Where a substantial degree of such turnover exists, the implication for the media planner in formulating objectives is that reach tends to take precedence over frequency and continuity since there will always be an influx of significant numbers of new prospects becoming part of the target audience for the first time.

Guidelines for Stating Media Objectives

Now we turn to the practical matter of how to get media objectives down on paper. What should be included and in how much detail? How should media objectives be expressed? Although different goals require varying degrees of supplementary information and/or supporting rationales, the media objectives themselves should be as brief as possible. Since most thorough media plans will include a section on background material or appendices expounding on the media objectives, short statements of objectives (a single sentence may suffice) provide a good overview of what the entire plan is designed to accomplish.

The following discussion highlights areas in which stated media objectives are most often necessary. Each area is briefly explained and then followed by an exemplary media objective for hypothetical Brand C, a dry cat food in its third year of national marketing. Brand C has a distribution level of 75 to 85 percent, making it comparable to competing national brands in the dry cat food product category. Brand C has good market share, and is one of the major advertisers in the category, but is not the market leader.

Target Audience Definition

A succinct definition of the target audience is probably the most important element in the media plan's statement of objectives. If applicable, relative emphasis on a primary versus a secondary target audience should also be stated.

BRAND C MEDIA OBJECTIVE: Concentrate message delivery towards current users of dry cat food, with primary emphasis on women, age 25 to 54, who live in metro city and suburban areas, and who have household incomes of $20,000 + . The psychographic profile includes current users of Brand C who have high emotional involvement with their cats, consider their cats as a good friend or companion, and take pride in and get satisfaction from their cats.

Creative Requirements

The interrelationships between creative requirements and media planning mean that, in stating media objectives, consideration must be given to the nature of potentially desirable creative strategies and executions.

BRAND C MEDIA OBJECTIVE: Provide a positive and quality environment that offers the opportunity to portray the emotional involvement between the owner and the cat.

Reach and Frequency

In preparing a media plan for evaluation, reach and frequency goals should usually be outlined, but occasionally these goals might not be stated outright as media objectives. Consider, for example, a proposed media plan in which a 65 percent reach and 8.0 frequency may be as equally desirable as a 75 percent reach and 7.0 frequency. Although precise reach/frequency goals might not be stated as media objectives, this would not diminish the importance of reach and frequency as key criteria by which the adequacy of the media plan would be judged. Estimated reach and frequency must at least be included in the media schedule. However, in all matters of reach/frequency goals—whether explicitly stated as media objectives or handled in some other way—it is important for the planner to consider alternative approaches which could, in fact, be better for the brand.

BRAND C MEDIA OBJECTIVE: Achieve a minimum level of 80% reach against the target audience with an average frequency of 3.0 over an average four-week period.

Timing

Although continuous advertising versus flighting and pulsing is a strategic question, the strategy chosen must be derived from media objectives that describe how marketing considerations affect the way messages should be delivered to the target audience over a particular period of time. When applicable, the following factors (discussed previously) should be addressed in stating media objectives that pertain to timing influences:

- Seasonal sales skews
- Product life cycle
- Repurchase cycle
- Competitive advertising patterns

(For the purpose of offering an exemplary objective, only the timing influence most critical to Brand C is treated below.)

BRAND C MEDIA OBJECTIVE: Maintain competitive weight levels throughout the year in an effort to work in conjunction with flat seasonality.

Geography

Media objectives should also outline how the geographical aspects of both the brand's distribution and media alternatives will be addressed. State whether national or local media will be used, or whether local media will be used to balance the geographical fluctuations in national media delivery. If there are any differences between geographic coverage in proposed media and geographic distribution for the brand, such differences should be taken into account.

BRAND C MEDIA OBJECTIVE: Develop a plan with even weight nationally to support Brand C's national marketing efforts.

Special Marketing Problems

Occasionally, marketing objectives reflecting special marketing problems require the support of specific media executions. When such a situation exists, a stated media objective describing that support may be appropriate.

A marketing objective for a cat food producer, for example, might be to maintain previous levels of brand trial in the wake of substantial target market turnover. That objective reflects the special marketing problem of large numbers of consumers becoming first-time prospects during the period covered by the marketing plan. The derivative advertising objective is to offer a trial-inducing incentive in advertising messages. The ability to implement effectively a strategy to fulfill that objective rests on the selection of media that are, for instance, capable of carrying a cents-off coupon.

BRAND C MEDIA OBJECTIVE: Coordinate media scheduling with major promotional events (free standing inserts and Sunday supplements) in order to maximize the total marketing effort.

Budget

Often it is a good idea to complete the statement of media objectives within the context of the amount of money being used. This provides each reader of the media plan with a complete picture of the situation at the plan's outset.

BRAND C MEDIA OBJECTIVE: Achieve all of the above objectives as efficiently as possible within the overall media budget of $7,000,000.

Once you have written out the media objectives, reread them to be sure that they tell what you want to do rather than how to do it. If a statement prescribes "how to," chances are you've written a strategy statement instead of an objective.

The Importance of Specificity in Media Objectives

Just as marketing planners have learned the value of making their sales goals and marketing communication goals specific, media planners must recognize the worth of stating media objectives as quantitatively as possible. In addition to discouraging the planner from leaning on meaningless and vague media generalities, employing specificity in written statements of media objectives serves two main purposes: (1) it provides benchmarks against which the performance of the media schedule can be evaluated and (2) it gives direction to the process of selecting alternative media vehicles.

Granted, the ability to quantify media goals rests heavily on the availability of research and management's willingness to invest in securing more detailed information about the media environment. Goals of almost any nature could be quantified, but the cost of gathering the information necessary to do so is often prohibitive. It is relatively easy to quantify reach and frequency objectives since both are measures that are ultimately dealt with in quantitative terms. But consider, for example, the more difficult question of how we may quantify media goals that pertain to competitive approach.

Suppose you are introducing a new brand into a product category that has a firmly entrenched market leader. As many marketers do in similar situations, you decide to avoid a head-on confrontation with that leader and, instead, opt for capturing a neglected market segment. Part of the very confrontation that you wish to avoid is a media confrontation, in which your ads appear in the same vehicles as the leader's ads. Thus, the general crux of your media goal with respect to competitive approach would be to select media vehicles that minimize the level of direct noise, or directly competitive messages within the same vehicle. It's easy to stop there, but this goal can be quantified to provide meaningful direction for media buying activities. Specifically, the media objectives might be stated as follows: "to select media vehicles which carry an amount of directly competitive messages ≤ 1." This tells media buyers to reject space, for instance, in any magazine issue carrying more than one directly competitive message. The new brand's media environment can thus be improved if the brand's marketers are willing to expend the research effort necessary to insure that implementation of the media plan is consistent with the stated objective.

This illustration was inserted simply to show that qualitative media objectives can often be taken a step further toward greater specificity. Whenever the potential enhancement of advertising performance stands to outweigh the cost of research, the media planner should insist on taking that extra step. The result can only be a more scientific media plan.

Summary

This chapter was designed to help you understand the nature of media objectives and the important influences on those objectives. Along the way you have become acquainted with the three concepts most basic to media planning: reach, frequency, and continuity. Gross rating points were also briefly explained.

Be forewarned that media terminology tends to be inconsistent across marketing and advertising literature, so before proceeding to the next chapter, be sure that you understand these terms in the context in which they were presented.

You were reminded in this chapter that reach, frequency and continuity cannot all be maximized in the same media schedule. The media planner must determine priorities, and we have offered some general guidelines for making that determination. Factors which serve as such guidelines include product life cycle, breadth of target market, repurchase cycle and target market turnover. Yet, these guidelines are not intended as foolproof keys to successful media planning in every situation; rather, they must be considered in light of many other situational variables. And don't forget that going against the traditional rules-of-thumb has often proven an effective strategy for adventuresome marketers willing to go out on a limb.

Once media objectives have been thought out, they must be stated in the media plan. Some suggestions and examples were offered on how to approach the task of writing statements of media objectives.

Finally, the importance of quantifying media objectives to the fullest practical extent was discussed. In recalling that strategy and tactics are derived from objectives, it logically follows that specific objectives make for more efficient implementation of the media plan.

Endnotes

1. For a discussion of some of the things known about repetition, see Leo Bogart, *Strategy in Advertising,* 2nd edition (Lincolnwood: Crain Books/NTC Business Books, 1984), pp. 207-234.

2. See John S. Wright, et al., *Advertising,* 5th edition (New York: McGraw-Hill Book Co., 1982), pp. 315-316.

3. For a discussion of this formula, advanced by James O. Peckham of the A. C. Nielsen Company, see Leo Bogart, *Strategy in Advertising,* 2nd edition (Lincolnwood: Crain Books/NTC Business Books, 1984). pp. 45-47.

Chapter Five

The Media Mix and Media Weighting Decisions

We have emphasized throughout this text that strategy is derived from objectives. Decisions regarding the media mix—that is, what balance of media types will be used over a given period of time—are strategy considerations and therefore should logically flow from established media objectives.

To illustrate, suppose you are a planner working toward the fulfillment of a media objective that specifies a need for a high level of reach. A strategy often employed in such a situation is one of making allocations to an assortment of two or more types of media. For example, you may decide that you can best extend your reach by employing a plan that results in spending 40% of the budget on network television, 40% on newspapers, and 20% on spot radio.

If, however, you are devising a strategy to attain a media objective that emphasizes a high frequency requirement, you may want to pound the message home with the impact you can get from concentrating all your ad dollars in a single media type. The rationale for using each type of media mix, concentrated or assorted, is discussed later in this chapter.

Media Weighting

Media planners must decide at the strategy level how advertising effort will be allocated in terms of target markets (primary, secondary, etc.), geographic regions, timing, and, of course, media types. Budget allocation in each of these areas is a matter of *relative emphasis;* that is, ''weighting'' decisions are concerned with how much emphasis, or weight, should be applied to each target, each region, each time segment, and each media type.

Weighting by Target Market

The weighting decision as it pertains to target markets transcends the boundaries of the media planning function as such and is more properly viewed as a marketing consideration. In chapter three, we discussed primary markets, secondary markets, and so on. A typical dual-market situation is one in which a child is the actual user of the product but the parent is the purchasing agent. To arrive at a weighting decision, the marketer must ask, ''What is the relative value of each of these targets (children and parents) in terms of what I want to accomplish with my marketing strategy?''

To help answer this question, research data exist for many products which describe the user's influence on the purchasing agent's decision to buy. In cases where such information does not exist or is outdated, it may be worthwhile to invest in the research necessary to find it out. In deciding what portion of the media effort should be directed at each target, planners must rely on a good deal of subjective judgment, for this decision rests heavily upon the nature of buying influences that are not well understood even by consumer behavior experts.

Weighting by Geographic Region

The media effort should also be weighted by geographic region and a carefully thought out and detailed marketing plan goes a long way toward helping the media planner make the geographic weighting decision. Geographic weighting requires the flexibility provided by local media. The media planner must make a judgment as to whether geographical sales fluctuations or geographic variations in media delivery are substantial enough to warrant the added expense of buying time/space on a local basis.

A good marketing plan will provide specific sales objectives by territory for each brand. These objectives, along with the scope of the brand's distribution system, are crucial keys to determining what portion of the advertising budget should be allocated to media in each geographic area. After all, the media planner's function is planning the purchase of advertising time and space in such a way that he maximizes its contribution to the attainment of sales goals.

Sometimes the matter of weighting by geographic region is further complicated by the fact that national media deliver to each region at different levels. Let's illustrate this situation with an example.[1] Assume your brand is sold in five regions of the United States and you want to allocate a $20 million budget to network and spot television (keep in mind that spot television is bought on a market-by-market basis). Your goal is to spend in each region in proportion to the sales potential. Further, you have checked with the networks to determine their audience deliveries in your regions. The differentials in network delivery to regions can be "balanced" by using spot television. The following table shows how such a budget allocation might be made:

Region	Sales Potential	Network Delivery	Budget Goal (based on sales potential)	Budget Allocation Network TV	Spot TV
1	15%	10%	$ 3,000,000	$ 1,142,857	$1,857,143
2	25	20	5,000,000	2,285,714	2,714,286
3	20	35	4,000,000	4,000,000	—
4	30	20	6,000,000	2,285,714	3,714,286
5	10	15	2,000,000	1,714,286	285,714
Total	100%	100%	$20,000,000	$11,428,571	$8,571,429

Thus, all of Region 3's budget is spent on network television because of the high degree of over-delivery. Other regions are balanced between network and spot.[2]

Weighting by Continuity/Timing Considerations

A media plan can only be executed after a decision is made as to what portion of the media effort will be allocated to time segments within the overall period covered by the media plan. Although the timing approaches of continuous advertising, pulsing, and flighting were defined in Chapter 4, a further look at their role in the media plan is especially relevant in a discussion of media weighting decisions. These concepts are the strategic outgrowths of decisions concerning "when the advertiser wants to be out there" with the message.

Any evaluation of the alternative strategies of continuous advertising, and flighting and pulsing should address the following considerations beyond the omnipresent budget constraints: (1) seasonal sales skews (2) repurchase cycle, (3) product life cycle, (4) competitive advertising patterns and level, (5) reach and frequency objectives, and (6) the desire to dominate a medium (relative to competition).

How the media effort is weighted by time segments can be seen in illustrations of continuous, flighting, and pulsing advertising schedules shown in Figures 5.1A, 5.1B, and 5.1C.

Thus, the continuous schedule involves spending about the same percent of the total budget each month, or 8 and one-third percent for a twelve-month plan. The flighting schedule shown indicates an expenditure of 20 percent in January, with lesser amounts in other months, and no media effort in March, April, and August. The pulsing schedule shows monthly spending throughout the yearly campaign period, ranging from 15 percent in May to 5 percent in each of five other months.

Figure 5.1A

Continuous Advertising Schedule

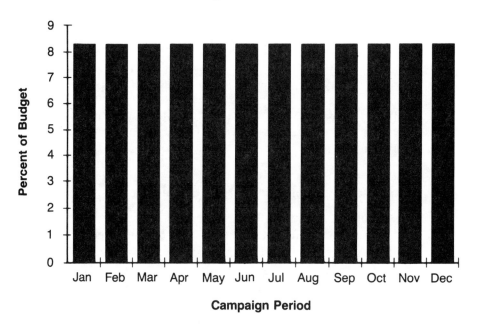

Figure 5.1B

Flighting Advertising Schedule

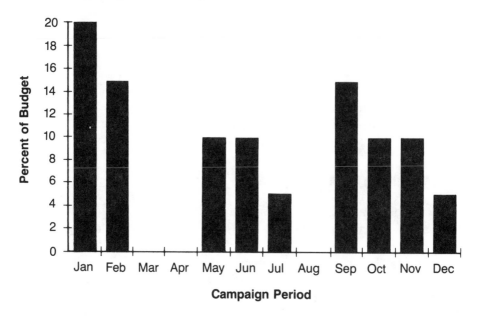

Figure 5.1C

Pulsing Advertising Schedule

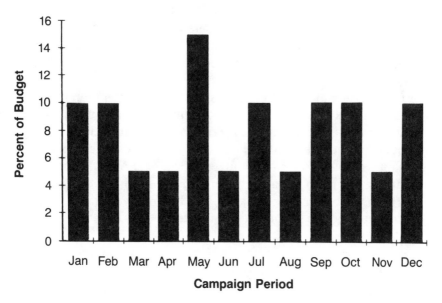

When more than one media type is used, the interrelationships between those media offer the opportunity to choose from more timing options, as illustrated by the schedules for an assorted media mix of television and magazines in Figures 5.2A and 5.2B.

Figure 5.2A shows that television (which is 60% of the total budget) and magazines (40%) are used in flighting patterns such that neither medium is used in March, June, July, or August. Figure 5.2B describes what might be called an *overlapping continuous/flighting schedule,* whereby one media type is used every month—so that the total plan is continuous—but each media type is flighted over the campaign period.

Weighting by Media Types

A fourth weighting decision arises when, given reach and frequency goals, the media planner chooses the strategy of employing an assorted mix of media types that have the most potential for fulfilling those goals. The planner must determine how much relative emphasis should be placed on each type of media in the assortment. Remember: since some media are much more expensive than others (on an absolute cost basis), the actual relative amounts of advertising delivered through each media type is seldom proportionate to the relative amounts of money invested in each type. Consider, for example, two simple assortments with identical budgets. In assorted mix A, exactly half the budget is allocated to newspapers and half to television. In mix B, half the budget is also allocated to newspapers, but the other half is invested in radio. Although the same percentage of the budget (and hence, the same amount of money) is allocated to newspapers in both mixes, there is more relative emphasis on newspapers in mix A since the other half of the budget will purchase far less time in television than in radio. (Although this example is discussed in terms of relative budget emphasis, relative media effectiveness in terms of communication or reach and frequency is not to be inferred, because effectiveness depends on many variables above and beyond budget allocation.) Again, subjective judgment plays an important role in this weighting decision, and the overriding consideration must always be how well the vehicles within any media type can be matched to the target markets.

Figure 5.2A

Exclusive Flighting Schedule

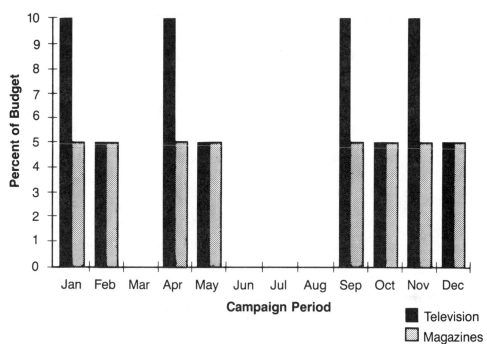

Figure 5.2B

Overlapping Continuous/Flighting Schedule

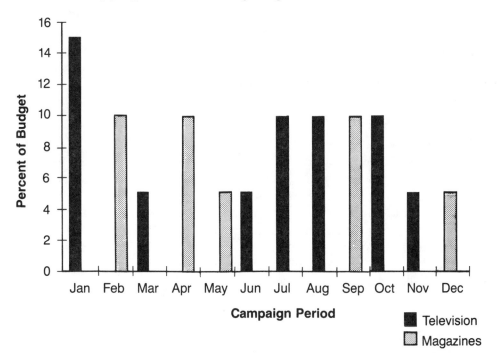

Shifting Media Mix

Regardless of how well an advertising campaign is performing, media planners may be tempted to speculate on whether a shift in media strategy—in the form of pulling out of one media type in favor of entering another, either during the campaign period or over a longer period of time—might give advertising results a boost. The following hypothetical situation should serve to point out the logic behind such a shift.

Suppose that the media schedule for an electric shaver campaign includes spot television in the top 25 markets and two national magazines with primarily male readership, such as *Sports Illustrated* and *Playboy*. But let's say that half-way through the campaign period, a decision is made to pull out of television and instead get into radio in those top 25 markets. For a time after the shift, in addition to whatever results the advertiser gets from the messages in radio and magazines, there will also be a benefit from the carryover effects of the television spots that ran during the first half of the campaign and consumers may experience the feeling that advertising for the product has been increased.

Shifting the mix during a campaign period can, however, be a very dangerous tack, and you should be aware of its pitfalls. It takes a substantial period of time to gain the full measure of potential effectiveness that one medium has to offer. Also, by sticking within the context of the same media types throughout the campaign period, the advertiser stands to establish a rapport with the prospect. In addition to reducing the level of pure repetition of the message, too much shifting can cause the advertiser to fail to establish that rapport and may in fact cause consumers to be confused by having to cope with unfamiliar message contexts throughout the campaign.

Media Mix Strategies

As previously mentioned, a media mix may be concentrated with all ad dollars invested in one media type, or it may be assorted, with ad dollars allocated among different media types. There typically is not a best strategy approach for an advertiser to take in any given situation. The planner must examine a broad array of marketing and advertising factors to arrive at a decision that works best for the brand at a particular time. Following is a discussion of the rationales behind both strategies.

Rationale for a Concentrated Mix

Concentration allows the advertiser to gain great impact on a specific audience segment, and in this advantage lies the most basic rationale underlying such a strategy. Under certain conditions, concentration may also allow the advertiser to dominate one medium relative to his competition. The added benefit of brand familiarity can accrue to this strategy, especially among consumers who have a narrow range of media exposure. This phenomenon is explained by Leo Bogart:

> The advertiser who pursues this course expects that his strong impact on a part of the market is translated into greater familiarity with his brand—and thus to actual preference. When it is hard for him (the consumer) to distinguish brands in actual use, he is likely to select the brand he perceives as most familiar and acceptable. He may identify the brand's apparent popularity with public approval, which in turn he associates with successful performance. It must be the best if it's the favorite! The sharply concentrated use of a single medium can give a brand this aura of mass acceptance in the eyes of people whose restricted orbit of media exposure coincides with the advertiser's scheduling strategy.[3]

Concentrating ad dollars, especially in big media buys such as premium television programming and ad sections in magazines, offers the advantage of creating excitement in the distribution channel. When a manufacturer can tell dealers, "We have purchased a TV mini-series to help you sell our brand," the dealers find prestige in having their customers associate them with that brand. The excitement that is engendered by such a media buy tends to motivate channel members to increase their level of support for the brand.

Within a media type, concentrating ad dollars in a single vehicle also has important benefits. An advertiser who pursues this course can expect better merchandising and promotional support from the vehicle chosen, as well as better discounts and preferential positioning. Each media type holds unique opportunities for advertisers who subscribe to a strategy of concentration. Special sections in magazines, for example, not only give the advertiser a chance to tell an entire product story, but also offer a way to promote a full line of products under one manufacturer's umbrella. And television mini-series protect the sponsor from competing TV commercials for the duration of the program.

Rationale for an Assorted Mix

Many advertisers find that concentration is not the best route to travel, for an assorted media mix offers significant advantages that are indeed difficult to pass up. An assorted mix facilitates audience segmentation by allowing the advertiser to deliver different messages through different media to different kinds of people. This opportunity is an especially important plus for advertisers who have more than one target, and it explains why it is common for a marketer of children's products to employ an assorted mix that includes Saturday morning television to reach children and home service magazines to reach their parents.

Through an assorted mix, advertisers can communicate with the same prospects in different psychological contexts. It has been suggested that, if a message is presented in a variety of media environments, it will maintain the prospect's interest over a longer time span than if it were allowed to wear out in a single medium. There is also a learning implication here: the consumers may more readily learn the content of the message if it comes to them via different channels. This hypothesis, however, is not definitively supported by consumer behavior research.

An assorted mix is also advantageous in its tendency to favorably affect the media schedule's reach. With an assortment of media types, reach against the target market is usually extended beyond what can normally be achieved within the practical limits of one medium. Depending on media objectives, level coverage of an audience may be desired, and an assortment of media most always helps the advertiser meet that end. To illustrate, consider the advertiser who has invested in prime time network television and has attained a reach through that medium of 80%. This is overall reach, and one can further look at the television exposure situation in terms of different levels of TV viewing.

It is a fact that some TV households spend considerably more time watching television than do other households. We therefore have heavy viewer and light viewer segments among the television viewing population, and the frequency gained by the network TV buy is uneven across all viewers. For example, Figure 5.3 shows exposure among adults for prime time and fringe day parts. Adult viewers are divided into five levels of viewing (quintiles—or 20 percent segments). Thus, for prime time viewing, the 20 percent of adults who are the heaviest viewers account for 39.3% of total viewing, compared with the lightest viewers who account for only 3.1% of all viewing. Comparable figures for early and late fringe time periods are 47.1% and 1.7% respectively.

Figure 5.3

Comparison of TV Exposure Among All Adults, by Two Dayparts

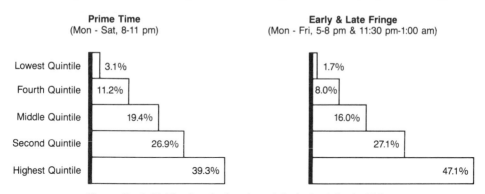

How to Read: 39.3% of total prime time adult viewing is by the highest quintile group (who account for 1/5 — or 20% — of all adults viewing)

Source: Data are from 1985 SMRB Study of Media & Markets

Now let's say that the advertiser changes to an assortment by adding magazines to the mix. Since heavy TV viewers tend to be light readers of magazines and light viewers tend to be heavy readers, reach among heavy and light viewers will become less disparate when magazines are added to the mix. We can see, then, that an assorted mix helps level the imbalances inherent in one medium.

Table 5.1 compares two alternative media mixes at the same budget levels, and illustrates the differences between the alternatives in terms of reach, average frequency, and frequency distribution.

In order to understand another set of conditions under which an assorted mix can be very effective, we must refer back to the rationale for concentration, in which we examined Leo Bogart's explanation of how concentration can enhance brand familiarity. You will recall that this phenomenon could only be expected to occur among prospects who have a narrow range of media exposure. But what of prospects whose range of media exposure is broad? For this group of individuals, concentrating the media effort might result in a situation whereby gaps are left in potential message exposure. Communicating through an assorted mix tends to develop brand image continuity among these prospects; that is, since a prospect's exposure to a variety of media indicates an intrinsic interest in a number of different areas, the advertiser may use an assortment of media to deliver the message within each of the prospect's spheres of interest.

Table 5.1

Reach and Frequency of Alternative Media Mixes (Women 25-54)

	Alternative A (TV Only)		Alternative B (TV and Magazines)	
• Reach & Frequency				
	R	F	R	F
TV.....................................	74.9%	4.3	72.8%	3.3
Magazines...........................	—	—	53.0	1.9
ALL MEDIA......................	74.9%	4.3	87.2%	3.9

• Total GRP's

322	340

• Frequency Distribution

F	R	F	R
1	17.2%	1	22.1%
2	13.3	2	16.5
3	10.2	3	12.3
4	7.9	4	9.2
5	6.1	5	6.9
6	4.7	6	5.1
7	3.6	7	3.8
8	2.8	8	2.9
9	2.1	9	2.1
10+	7.0	10+	6.3
	74.9%		87.2%

Source: Telmar Group Inc.

In reviewing considerations that may lead to recommending an assorted mix, the media planner should be alert to a potential disadvantage of using multiple media types. A mix of two or more media types requires that a larger portion of the total advertising budget be invested in the physical preparation of advertising materials, leaving a smaller portion available for purchasing time/space. When the investment in advertising production becomes a very significant portion of the total budget (media plus production), a warning signal is flashing to indicate that the media mix may be spread too thin.

Summary

This chapter has been concerned with the strategy considerations related to media mix decisions—those decisions regarding how the advertising effort should be allocated among media types. The media planner must make other media weighting decisions as well, including how much relative emphasis should be placed on each target market (where more than one target exists), each geographic area, and each time segment within the campaign period. These areas of decision making have broad marketing implications, and the pertinent media strategies should be carefully derived from the marketing plan.

It has often been hypothesized that shifting the media mix during a campaign period will give advertising results a boost. In this chapter we explored the advantages of this strategy as well as its possible repercussions. The shifting techniques can be effective under certain sets of circumstances, but when used the least bit carelessly, it can severely reduce the advertiser's potential for maximizing the effectiveness of each ad dollar.

Finally, this chapter dealt with two basic media mix strategies. In a concentrated mix, the advertiser invests all ad dollars in one media type. In an assorted mix, ad dollars are allocated among different types of media. The advantages of both approaches, as well as situations conducive to their applications, were discussed in some detail.

Endnotes

1. See S. W. Dunn and Arnold M. Barban, *Advertising: Its Role in Modern Marketing,* 6th edition (Chicago: The Dryden Press, 1986), pp. 382-383; also, Jack Z. Sissors and Jim Surmanek, *Advertising Media Planning,* 2nd edition (Lincolnwood: Crain Books/NTC Business Books, 1982), pp. 321-324.

2. See Dunn and Barban for the mathematical procedure to balance network and spot within regions.

3. Leo Bogart, *Strategy in Advertising,* 2nd edition (Lincolnwood: Crain Books/NTC Business Books, 1984), p. 147.

Chapter Six

Summary and Conclusions

The purpose of this concluding chapter is threefold: (1) to review and integrate the essentials of media planning as presented in this text, (2) to highlight the importance of sophisticated management tools, especially the computer, in media problem-solving, and (3) to stimulate thinking on the direction in which the media planning function is heading.

Review and Summarization

The essentials of media planning include not only the components of the planning function and the concepts employed in planning activities, but also external influences that affect the function. Integrating these components, concepts, and influences as we summarize them should help you to view media planning in its totality.

Chapter 1 prepared you for developing an understanding of the hierarchy of media decisions by differentiating between objectives, strategy, and tactics. A schematic overview showed the totality of the media decision-making process. Media planning was defined as the process of designing a course of action that shows how advertising time and space will be used to contribute to the achievement of marketing objectives. Implicit in that definition is the suggestion that any exploration into the nature of media planning should begin with a study of marketing, and this was precisely what was done in Chapter 2.

In considering media problems as a type of marketing problem, Chapter 2 dealt with how different elements of the marketing mix influence media planning. Because product characteristics, distribution channels, pricing strategy, promotion, and packaging provide such crucial inputs to media decisions, Chapter 2 showed why we cannot simply begin writing a media plan without first studying the marketing situation and the uncontrollable variables affecting that situation.

Chapter 3 introduced the most significant link between marketing planning and media planning: the target market. The entire marketing plan revolves around the target market, and the media planner's task is to deliver marketing messages to target prospects by matching media audiences to the target market description. The planner's ability to perform that task rests heavily on how definitively the marketing plan describes the target market in terms of demographic characteristics, sociopsychological variables, and/or levels of product usage.

With the marketing situation firmly in mind and a target market definition before us, we are ready to begin writing the media plan. Chapter 4 discussed the starting point for the plan: media objectives. The logic of Chapter 1 tells us that objectives must be carefully formulated to provide guidelines for evaluating strategy alternatives. You were introduced to the concepts of reach, frequency, and continuity to prepare you for dealing with media objectives in meaningful terms and were offered guidelines for formulating and actually stating these objectives.

Chapter 5 ventured into the realm of media strategy by discussing considerations related to media mix and other media weighting decisions. The discussion outlined basic strategy alternatives between which media planners must inevitably choose. Some clues to aid the planner in making those choices were also provided.

In conclusion, then, we have started with broad marketing considerations and funneled our way down through the hierarchic sequence of decision-making areas, stopping at the tactical level.

Media Decisions Today and Tomorrow: Application of Management Tools

As media planning becomes more disciplined, interest grows in new management tools that may enhance the effectiveness with which marketing dollars are invested in advertising time and space. The computer is one important tool that has already found a significant niche in the world of media decision-making. In developing a basic understanding of media planning and strategy, it is not essential that one study the intricacies of computerized media selection. As a media planner, however, it is extremely useful to understand the capabilities and benefits of the computer's application to media problems. Through such an understanding, planners will know what can reasonably be expected from a computerized system.

Let us first consider computer capabilities in very basic terms. The computer aids decision-making through its ability to rapidly screen and evaluate thousands of different levels of reach and frequency as well as targeting data describing those reached. By identifying alternative media plans in the event that the advertising budget is cut or increased, the computer is able to make another important contribution to the planning function.

Based on the target market selected for a given product, the computer ultimately indicates the most efficient combination of media alternatives and can even print out comparisons between other plans and the one selected as most efficient. Thus, the computer aids us by providing optimum solutions to media problems—that is, it tells us not only what is feasible within specified budget constraints, but also what is best in terms of the variables with which it deals.

Many sophisticated media planners are using mathematical media models to which their computers are programmed.[1] Such models are capable of yielding media schedules which maximize a certain desired characteristic; for example, the number of men, ages 35-49, with incomes of $25,000 or more, who are reached at least twice every four weeks within the specified budget constraints.

Although many advertisers and agencies maintain an interest in utilizing their own media models and in-house computing facilities, perhaps more have turned recently to the use of outside media analysis services. For example, Telmar Group Inc. and IMS (Interactive Marketing Systems) provide an array of services that facilitate the media function. Through the use of microcomputers on-site in an agency's media department, the media planner accesses (by telephone lines) the service's mainframe computer where industry data bases (such as SMRB and MRI) and analytical media programs are available.

Telmar recently developed an adaptation of their earlier time-sharing system. Some of the features of their new approach—called MICRO-NETWORK II[SM] —follow.

- Users can perform all analysis on the micro, link their personal computers into local area networks, automatically access the vast data in Telmar's mainframe computers, and at the same time provide gateway to any data supplier's mainframe.
- Users can get time-oriented budgeting, flow charting, reach-and-frequency estimates for all media, and instantaneously retrieve literally hundreds of media plans and proposals.
- Users can have a whole plan electronically costed, summarized, analyzed for reach-and-frequency, printed, and filed for future reference and ''what if'' analysis.
- Users can interface with full color graphics programs for plotting or for client presentation.

We thus find an array of new management tools available to the media planner of today and tomorrow. Yet, we must caution that, regardless of the sophistication of computer technology in dealing with media issues, many decisions come down to judgment—the human element in media decision-making. As media expert Richard C. Anderson said, "planners will always have to modify computer printouts with a great deal of personal judgment," and he went on to point out four unanswerable questions.[2]

1. A computer cannot tell the planner which medium is most suitable for the message. . . .
2. The computer cannot analyze environments of media and tell which is best for the message being disseminated. . . .
3. The computer cannot tell the planner when to switch to some other medium. . . .
4. The computer cannot tell the planner how to reach the consumers with an unexpected message in an unexpected place. . . .

The Marriage of Media and Marketing

Media planning and marketing are growing closer together, so that any sharp distinctions which may have existed between them are becoming increasingly blurred. We find evidence of this welcome coalescence on both sides of the advertising fence, among agencies and clients alike. Media departments in advertising agencies are tending to function as marketing departments. On the client side, the use of the brand management system has fostered a situation in which the managers who participate in media decision making are the same people that have their fingers on the total marketing pulse from day to day. The *Marketing & Media Decisions* article that appears on the following pages should be interesting to the reader.

In light of the premise of this text—that media problems are marketing problems and should be approached accordingly—this fusion of media planning and marketing is indeed a healthy situation. The marketing viewpoint should help media planning become a more efficient function, and less waste of advertising dollars will benefit both the producers and consumers of goods and services.

Endnotes

1. For a discussion of media models, see Jack Z. Sissors and Jim Surmanek, *Advertising Media Planning,* 2nd edition (Lincolnwood: Crain Books/NTC Business Books, 1982), pp. 356-362, and Leo Bogart, *Strategy in Advertising,* 2nd edition (Chicago: Crain Books, 1984), pp. 333-347.

2. Richard C. Anderson, as quoted in Sissors and Surmanek, *Advertising Media Planning,* p. 377.

Toying with how to wed marketing with media

Rebecca Fannin

With clients pushing for more intelligent media buys, agencies see a greater need for media departments to be a vital link in the client's overall marketing strategy. But some clients prefer agencies just to execute media buys.

I t's a struggle as clear as the tug between old and new, weak and strong, power players versus defenders of the status quo. The object of the attention is the media department and the changing nature of its role within the agency and with clients.

Marketing has taken center stage with companies who are absorbed by the challenge of selling profitability in a fragmented, chokingly competitive environment. As such, they are questioning all aspects of their marketing, including whether advertising messages are being relayed to the right consumers using the right medium and whether the media plan *furthers* the overall marketing objective.

The situation has some advertisers demanding that their agency's media department take a stronger hand in marrying media usage to marketing strategies. Other clients, used to developing their own marketing programs, argue that agency participation that goes beyond creating ads and executing media buys is an unproven need. And somewhere in between, are a growing group of clients who, concerned over the rising costs of media,

the growing complexity of media alternatives and the birth of targeted marketing to an individualistic society, are expanding their own in-house media departments.

The import of this atmosphere is hardly lost on agency chiefs—or ambitious media directors. Creating a stronger link between marketing and media is winning greater support from agencies who see opportunities for growth by building strong media departments.

These agencies are challenging their media planners and buyers to think more like marketers and look beyond blind cost-per-thousand analysis. Where reach and frequency, efficiency and effectiveness used to be the gospel for media people, quality has become the new religion. Pointing out that subjective judgments are replacing quantifiable decisions is William E. Phillips, chairman and ceo of Ogilvy & Mather. "What's important today is the *value* per consumer reached," he stresses.

The transformation of the media discipline is sparking the emergence of a media person who can not only deci-

Rebecca Fannin, "Toying With How To Wed Marketing With Media," *Marketing & Media Decisions,* June 1985, pp. 60-64.

pher minute cost advantages between late fringe and early morning television spots, but a trained thinker who can intuitively understand the difference between marketing a shampoo to a glamour girl or to an intelligent, active woman who indulges in health and beauty needs, says Laurel Cutler, vice chairman of Leber, Katz. "We don't want media people who say they only do windows," she emphasizes.

Predictably, the distinct line between these branches of thought has begun to blur. Now that the personal computer can cough up cost-run analysis in seconds, media buyers theoretically have time and energy to incorporate marketing intelligence into more creative and astute media buys. And media planners, who are seeing buyers invade their domain, are also able to look beyond their traditional turf. With the computer making it easier to weigh planning options, there is greater freedom to become broader marketing people, perhaps even, crowding the role of account service manager. Art Wilen, senior vice president, development and professional services at Interpublic, believes the lines of responsibility have become so hazy that "a new character will evolve, a business development manager who handles both media and marketing."

BBDO already has established a new unit called the diversified communications group which extends the media department's services into marketing disciplines such as promotion, specialized markets, research and video development. Others such as Benton & Bowles have made media a team player with high level groups of creative, research, media and account managers who work on one account. And even smaller agencies with strong marketing backgrounds such

as Leber Katz have set up a special post that marries marketing research with media.

In addition, several large agencies have tried to emphasize marketing clout possible in media placement by assigning responsibility for local market purchases to media buyers in regional offices or a centralized staff with greater familiarity of area nuances. For instance, Detroit's Campbell-Ewald has restructured its media department and abandoned the practice of using media specialists for spot buying in favor of "local market specialists." These buyers are each responsible for purchasing newspapers, radio, tv, outdoor and magazines in a market. The agency hopes this approach will lead to a more coordinated and comprehensive message plus increase presence for its clients. (For more, see "Buying Topeka: Campbell-Ewald's solution," on page 52.)

Pressure to strengthen the media department is, in part, defensive. Media has traditionally suffered from a step-child syndrome, but media inflation and intriguing new options have heightened client interest in media investments. Advertisers are adding to advertising/marketing staffs to monitor advertising's effectiveness, challenging agencies with the possibility that their increased knowledge could lead to an account taken in-house and lost. While most agencies and advertisers argue that their relationship is a partnership, the heat is on ad agencies to keep up with clients.

"Not too long ago, many of the corporate ad directors you would work with were salesmen that had gotten too old to go on the road; they just took poor Charlie and let him be the ad person," says Richard J. Lord, chairman and chief executive officer at Lord,

Geller, Federico, Einstein. "But, with the money it costs to get into the game of advertising, companies are hiring more intellectual and curious people."

Mindful that stronger client watchdogs could shift the power balance between agency and advertiser, agency managements are promoting media departments' visibility and clout. "There is an ever-increasing appreciation of media," says Allen Rosenshine, chairman and chief executive officer of BBDO. "With the escalating cost of tv and growth of media alternatives, agencies have become far more cognizant of helping advertisers compete with extra value buys that heighten their brand image," he affirms.

But how much marketing support advertisers want from their agencies vacillates to a large degree. Explains Ogilvy & Mather's Phillips: "There is a whole segment of clients that really don't want their agencies involved in marketing. They want advertising agencies to do great ads. There's another whole segment—and I think this is the packaged goods segment—which generally does want their agencies involved in the marketing. They feel that with this involvement comes an understanding of copy and media needs."

But often, advertisers are not willing to work with agencies to ensure such demands can be met. Instead, agencies are treated as vendors, says Chicago-based consultant BarBara Bools. "They look to agencies for media in particular because that's the only thing they can't do," she notes.

When left out of the development process, ad agencies, however, can complain bitterly. "We had one client who wouldn't share sales figures so we could help them. They said, 'We do our own marketing, you just do the ads,' recalls Lord. "We took them up to the roof and threw them off." he says of the unnamed client who took the account in-house.

The situation is indeed frustrating, for what is often said in one breath is exhaled with the next. Gillette, for instance, "likes to have its agencies as marketing partners," according to Thomas J. Ryan, vice president of advertising services. But Ryan, who has helped to lead the company in a three year-old decision to boost targeted marketing expenditures, believes that only account and creative people should be involved in marketing strategy development. Media, he believes, "is more of an executional thing. It is involved in the development phase in pointing out reach and frequency."

The Chrysler Corp., in addition, looks to its agency media departments to suggest unusual media events for greater impact, but these same people rarely meet with Chrysler marketing executives for input. The Detroit office managers of Chrysler's agencies meet with the company's marketing staff people twice a month and its agencies' presidents assemble once a month with Chrysler's executive marketing committee (which includes chairman Lee Iacocca). Only after the marketing strategy is reviewed by the agencies' executives and then approved by the client does media get involved. "That's advertising, not marketing," says Joseph A. Campana, Chrysler's vice president of marketing, who draws a sharp line between development and execution of marketing plans.

Other companies though, are more eager to ensure that marketing and media speak with one voice. The Pillsbury Co., for instance, recently appointed Ron Kos as director of advertising specifically because, as a former marketing executive, he can better evaluate how well a media plan corresponds to the marketing objective, according to Donald A. Osell, vice president of marketing. Still, Osell stresses the benefit of calling on "our agencies for their very capable media specialists."

Indeed, Pillsbury relies heavily on its agencies to be full marketing partners as well. A year ago, the company put into writing that it expects BBDO and Kenyon & Eckhardt to "understand our business and strategies, think broadly about our business, think ahead of us, and come up with innovative ideas, not just in copy and media."

The Clorox Co. has taken a similar tack. To ensure media plans and buys proceed on the same course as marketing direction, Robert Bolte, Clorox's director of media, has implemented a formal structure. Last year, he began running a pre-planning meeting with the agency account service, client brand management, agency media, and client media to "discuss marketing direction as a prerequisite for developing media plans," tells Bolte. The annual meeting is designed to "share knowledge with the agency media folks," says Bolte, who adds the exchange is necessary for better productivity. "A brand manager might say to his staff that he wants to increase trial among non-users, but when the media person starts probing, he may find that there is a lack of selectivity of media, or the audience is too small or you can't measure it," he elaborates.

Striking the right balance between having media specialists on the one hand and marketing generalists on the other is difficult for ad agency media directors who face clients as diverse

as Gillette and Pillsbury in their needs and temperaments.

Some ad agency media directors such as Alec Gerster, executive vice president of media and programming at Grey, prefer their departments to concentrate on the traditional role in getting the most efficient buy. "Our job is to buy cost per thousands," he states. "I don't want an undisciplined judgment by 30 media specialists in the marketing area." At Grey, says Gerster, media buyers "are trained to bring in the lowest possible buy." They report to associate media directors who conduct post-analysis to ensure that it corresponds to the marketing strategy. Marketing information is gleaned through the product group concept which is staffed by the associate and other key executives from creative, research and account work, says Gerster.

But in today's power play world, more aggressive approaches are increasingly common. For example, BBDO has brought its new diversified communications group under the umbrella of the media department.

"The idea is that for the first time we are coordinating promotion, specialized markets such as Blacks and Hispanics, and video development under one umbrella and I run the umbrella organization as well as running media and programming," outlines Arnie Semsky, executive vice president, media director, network programming at BBDO. "What we have done is extend our media operation. We have also gotten the agency involved in business clients normally wouldn't look for from an agency," he says.

Even though the formalized structure was set up in February and is still being sold to additional BBDO U.S. offices, clients are responding positively. Semsky reports that the new group was instrumental in winning the Visa account. Another, unnamed account is in the wings. While the setup has not been tested for any account yet, Semsky believes that the tie-in between media and promotional services alone is key. "We've always felt that the more we could coordinate these messages, the more impact our overall message would have to the consumer and trade," he explains. "For instance, we would increase media expenditures when we knew promotional events were planned."

But BBDO's new group is also seen as an opportunistic move to generate new business.

Sold on a fee basis for the incremental work, BBDO's Rosenshine regards the group as a profit center, although he doesn't want to speculate on its potential for increased revenues. "We expect it will pay for itself, he allows, of the new group which is coordinated by project directors who work through BBDO's account groups.

Other agencies may not have taken such a drastic measure to meld marketing with media, but many have seen fit to create high level teams who work on one account from the specialized areas of creative, research, media and account management.

Ogilvy & Mather is one agency pleased with this group concept. "Because there is a small group working on one account, it is easier to get a team spirit," says Ken Caffrey, senior vice president, executive director of media operations. "Beyond that, it allows a focus on the client and helps to speed the advertising process."

But importantly, Caffrey indicates that the group concept has helped "to heighten awareness of media involvement by allowing inter-departmental participation in the development of strategy for the client." The team, which was set up a year ago after being used successfully in the London office, is now operating for approximately 75% of Ogilvy's New York clients.

Benton & Bowles also has seen fit to create a core group that links key people from creative, research and account service with media to "develop long-term strategy," says Phil Guarascio, senior vice president, director of media and management. "We are much more involved with development of the strategic process in defining prospects as we move into market segmentation," notes Guarascio.

Leo Burnett also has grouped media more closely with a similar setup. A media review committee including high-level media, research and client service managers meets to ensure that marketing input is coordinated with planning and execution of media, notes Bill Hadlock, executive vice president of the media services division. In addition, the agency seeks to further media's association with marketing by assigning media planning and buying to media directors who are members of the media review committee. "Unlike other media directors, ours are both planners and buyers. This way, we don't have buyers who can only negotiate network television buys. Instead, our buyers know more about the plan," says Hadlock.

Even at smaller agencies, where communication is presumably easier, the push is on to improve the link between marketing and media. Leber Katz has set up a communications planning group which unites marketing research with media. Nancy Posternack, a senior vice president who was recruited two years ago to set up the formal structure, notes that the group has become successful because it helps the two disciplines to work as "bedfellows on a brand by brand basis which brings more continuity to the business."

The effect of the communications planning group has been to allow input from complicated research methods into media decision making. For example, such research techniques as determining high volume users and attitudes of consumer product purchasers have been wedded with development of media plans for several clients. In the case of Pantene shampoo, the group decided after analyzing the target audience that they needed a broader media mix than the women's service books usually bought for Pantene. Since they discovered that Pantene shampoo users are active socially and concerned with nutrition and fitness, and not just beauty, a media schedule which included fashion, lifestyle, and city magazines was chosen.

Even though some forward thinkers believe that such cohesiveness could lead to fewer specialty functions and even eventually eliminate some roles such as account service, agency media directors don't necessarily agree.

"I'd like to meet the person who can both plan and buy media, and also meet all the demands placed on account service management," says Marianne Caponnetto, vice president, media director at Lord, Geller, Federico, Einstein.

"Somebody's got to pull it all together; somebody has to be appointed to be the coordinator for marketing, media, creative and billings for the client," she says.

Benton & Bowles' Guarascio points out the most important aspect of account management is in spearheading creative. "There are some people who suppose that marketing and media working together will get rid of account management, but I am not so much of a media chauvinist to believe that we don't have distinct boundaries," says Guarascio.

Improved marketing research, of its own volition, however, is bringing media closer to being a science than ever before. For instance, Ted Bates has recently signed a deal with Simmons Market Research Bureau for customized consumer buying behavior data that it believes will greatly enhance its media capabilities. This added research capability, pinpointing product categories with added consumer behavior values, is seen as a step toward marketing/media integration. "It will have enormous impact in linking marketing with media," exclaims Larry Light, executive vice president. "It will affect, through knowledge of attitudes, what programs and magazines to buy."

Whether the trickling down of new marketing insights into media decisions is fast enough is the question. Although the media department is gaining clout, without the full support of advertisers, there is a risk that a media decision made in a vacuum can only lead to one more wasted dollar.

Appendix

Media Plans:

Apple Computers

BRK Electronics' Autostat

Dunlop "DDH" Golf Balls

General Foods' Jell-O Brand Gelatin

General Mills/Betty Crocker Frosting

MEDIA PLAN FOR APPLE COMPUTERS

Client/Product: Apple Computers
Agency: Chiat/Day

I. Target Market

The overall consumer target audience is Men 25-54, $35,000+ Household Income, College Graduate +. (Universe 4,541,000)

Rationale:
The target audience as defined by Apple Computer and based on their research includes three major groups. Matching them to media definitions, they are as follows:

Apple Definition	SMRB Definition
Big Business	Managers/Administrators $35,000+ Household Income Company Size 100+ Employees Universe: 2,415,000
Small Business/ Proprietors	Managers/Administrators/ Proprietors $35,000+ Household Income Company Size—100 Employees Universe: 2,971,000
Professional	Professional/Technical $35,000+ Household Income Universe: 6,262,000

The authors wish to express their deep appreciation to Bruce Mowery, Advertising & Sales Promotion Manager of Apple Computers Inc., for permission to publish this material, and to David Yoder of Chiat/Day for his cooperation.

II. Media Objectives

A. Overall Objectives

Work in conjunction with Apple's Corporate Advertising objectives to:

- Promote understanding of what a personal computer can do,
- Position Apple as *the* preferred brand of personal computer,
- Support individual Apple product offerings,
- Motivate prospects to visit an Apple dealer or to inquire for additional information.

B. Specific Objectives

1. Geographic Emphasis

Provide national support for all product groups.
Provide regional media heavy-up for promotions. Markets will be determined by dealer participation.

Rationale:
Apple Computer has dealers throughout the country in virtually every ADI.* Several dealer analyses have shown that Apple's dealer representation closely matches population size. At this stage of product development, it appears that national coverage best matches Apple's growth patterns. Spot market heavy-up for promotions encourages dealer involvement as was evidenced by the recent business promotion. Regional support will be determined by actual dealer participation.

2. Communication Goals

Emphasize effective reach during the growth stage of the category to establish Apple as the preferred brand and to generate response.
Effective reach goals are defined as follows:

Reach 75% of the target audiences six or more times during the purchase cycle (three month period).

Rationale:
Communication goals have been established on a 3 month purchase cycle because most industry data support a lengthy decision-making process. This is also in keeping with similarly

*Area of Dominant Influence. An exclusive geographic area of countries as defined by Arbitron, the audience rating service) in which the home market television stations achieve the dominant share of viewing. Used for planning, buying and evaluating television audiences.

priced consumer goods. Target prospects also seem to make 5-6 visits to more than one dealer which would support the premise of a lengthy purchase cycle.

Research on effective frequency has established that 3 exposures in a purchase cycle is the rule of thumb for generating awareness for most products like soft drinks and paper towels. We believe a personal computer's minimal exposure level is higher because of the intimidating and confusing nature of the product. Also it is a considered investment because of the price.

3. Timing

Place heavier media weight in Apple's 1st and 3rd quarters.

Rationale:
The 1st Quarter will see the launch of Apple's new campaign. In addition, Apple has been at comparatively low media weights during the 4th quarter of current fiscal year.
In the 3rd Quarter two new products will be introduced.

4. Creative Requirements

Consider creative and environmental factors which require long copy for product descriptions and which will augment Apple's positioning as the preferred brand of personal computer.
Use the following *print* units:

Page 4-Color Bleed
Spread 4-Color Bleed
Inserts
- 8-page Consumer
- 12-page Business
- 4-page Education
- 4-page Peripheral

Use the following *television* units:

30-seconds
60-seconds

Rationale:
The variety of creative units reflects the communication objectives Apple has established:

- Promote understanding of the product
- Support a variety of product offerings
- Motivate prospects to visit an Apple dealer or inquire for additional information via an 800 number

5. *Budget*

The preliminary media budget has been established at $27,000,000.

III. Media Strategy and Tactics

Corporate Identity Campaign

A. The strategy for the Corporate Identity Campaign is to use:

- Consumer Print Publications
- Network Television

The media tactics are to:

1. Use page 4-color bleed units in the first quarter. (Page black-and-white in the *Wall Street Journal*)
2. Schedule an 8-page insert on a limited schedule in November.
3. Use a mix of :30s and :60s for television weighted on an average of 80% GRPs for :30s, 20% GRPs for :60s.
4. Concentrate ad and commercial placement in those publications and programs which best cover and editorialize to the target audience.
5. Schedule network TV in 1st and 2nd quarters with the following weighting emphasis:

Quarter	% Weighting	Approx. Target GRPs
1st	60%	550-575
2nd	40%	395-420

PCS Division

B. The strategy for supporting the PCS Division is to use:

Hardware

- Consumer Print publications for the Business Campaign
- Enthusiast publications for Apple IIe, and Inside Apple
- Regional newspapers and Wall Street Journal for the various promotions

Software

- Enthusiast publications

The media tactics are to:

Business Campaign

1. Schedule a 12-page supplied insert in January in selected business publications.
2. Follow up insert with spread units (2-page, 4-color bleed) in expanded list of publications (page black and white for *Wall Street Journal*).
3. Schedule on alternate month basis except for the *Wall Street Journal,* which will be scheduled twice a month.

Apple IIe

Schedule a spread 4-color bleed in Enthusiast publications on an alternate month basis beginning February.

Promotions—Christmas

1. Schedule a 1200 line national ad to run four times from mid-November to mid-December.
2. Schedule 3 SAU size #6 ads in local market newspapers beginning late November.

Support for other promotions to be determined.

Inside Apple

1. Use a variety of ad sizes and ad content to be charged to the PCS, Peripheral and Accessories Divisions.
2. Schedule a page 4-color in enthusiast publications to feature accessories in November.
3. Schedule a spread 4-color in enthusiast publications in January. Ad will feature accessories and peripherals.
4. Schedule spread 4-color units to run alternate months for remainder of year. Ad subjects to be determined.

Software

1. Use a spread 4-color bleed in Enthusiast publications.
2. Schedule Enthusiast publications on a pulsed basis:

Nov/Dec—Heavy   June—Heavy
Jan/Feb—Light   July/Aug—Light
March—Heavy   Sept—Heavy
Apr/May—Light

Two New Product Introductions

C. The strategy for supporting the two new product introductions is to use:

- National consumer print
- Network Television

The media tactics are to:

1. Announce New Product #1 in January with 2-page black and white ads in the *Wall Street Journal* to be followed with spread 4-color bleed units in other publications beginning April.
2. Begin advertising for New Product #2 June 1 with a spread 4-color bleed unit.
3. Determine Network TV scheduling at a later date.

Peripherals and Accessories Divisions

D. The strategy for the Peripherals and Accessories Divisions is to use:

- Enthusiast publications via Inside Apple
- Enthusiast publications for other ads

The media tactics are as follows:

1. For Peripherals, schedule 4-page supplied insert in February and continue on alternate month basis.
2. For Accessories, schedule ½ page 4-color in Enthusiast publications on a quarterly basis beginning January.

Sales Division

E. The strategy for the Sales Division is to use Vertical Market publications for the following markets:

- Management Information Systems
- Office Management
- Incentive
- Education
- Science/Industrial/Engineering/Original Equipment Manufacturers (OEM)
- Training

The media tactics are:

1. Schedule a spread 4-color bleed as follows:
   a. *Management Information Systems*—Begin November and continue on alternate month basis.
   b. *Office Management*—Begin April and continue on an every other month basis.

     c. *Science/Industrial/Engineering/OEM*—Begin January and continue on alternate month basis.

     d. *Training*—Begin November and continue on alternate monthly basis.

  2. Schedule a page 4-color bleed as follows:

     a. *Incentive*—Begin October and continue on quarterly basis.

  3. Schedule a spread 4-color bleed and 4-page supplied insert as follows:

     a. *Education*—Begin with spreads in November and continue on alternate monthly basis through March. Schedule insert in May.

IV. Media Strategy Rationale

1. Consumer magazines and the *Wall Street Journal* provide:
   - National coverage
   - Target audience selectivity
   - Editorial enhancement opportunities
   - Space for long copy
   - Reproduction excellence in magazines

2. Network television provides:
   - National coverage
   - Intrusive media environment which dramatizes the message for creative impact via sight, sound and motion
   - Relative flexibility for flighting considerations
   - Method of building awareness quickly
   - Exciting media support for all Apple dealers

3. Vertical Market magazines provide:
   - National coverage
   - In-depth coverage of selected target groups
   - Space for long copy
   - Opportunity to use precise applications addressed to selected markets
   - "Shopping" frame of mind

4. Local newspapers provide:
   - Direct and localized support for dealers
   - Opportunity to list multiple dealer addresses
   - A shopping document which can be saved for future reference
   - A sense of urgency
   - Space to detail promotion facts and rules
   - Scheduling flexibility
   - Minimum lead time for production

Chiat/Day

Apple Computer Inc.
Media Flowchart

Division	$ (000)	$ (000)	Oct	Nov	Dec	Jan	Feb	Mar	Apr	May	June	July	Aug	Sept
Corporate Identity		7279.3												
Print	1444.7													
Insert	1784.6			▮										
Network TV	4050.0			▮	▮									
PCS		11359.8												
Business Insert	927.1													
Business Print	5812.1							▮						
Apple IIe	354.5						▮	▮				▮	▮	▮
Inside Apple	128.7													
Promotions	3644.3			XMAS			Small Business	To Be Determined						▮
Software	493.1													
New Product #1		2953.8												
Print	978.8													
Network TV	1975.0					XX			To Be Determined					▮
New Product #2		2884.5												
Print	909.5													
Network TV	1975.0										To Be Determined			▮
Peripherals		570.4												
Inside Apple	210.4						▮		▮					▮
Other Print	360.0													
Accessories Product		271.6												
Inside Apple	203.3													
Other Print	68.3													
Sales		1806.0												
MIS	250.4											▮	▮	▮
Office	83.5													
Incentives	119.3			▮	▮					▮				▮
Education	512.8													
Ind/OEM/Sci	757.5													▮
Training	82.5													▮
TOTAL MEDIA	27,125.4			$7,512.3			$6,178.0			$6,614.7			$6,820.4	

V. Media Performance

Full Year Reach & Frequency Men 25-54, $35,000 HHI College Graduate +

Universe:
4,541,000
2.8%

	GRPs	% REACH	AVERAGE FREQUENCY
Corporate			
Identity Print	577	95	6.1
Network TV	970	93	10.4
TOTAL CORPORATE	1547	95	16.3
Business			
Print	1344	95	14.1
New Product #1			
Print	173	74	2.3
Network TV	415	85	4.9
TOTAL	588	95	6.2
New Product #2			
Print	172	78	2.2
Network TV	415	85	4.9
TOTAL	587	95	6.2
Combined New Products			
Print	345	88	3.9
Network TV	830	93	8.9
TOTAL	1175	95	12.4
TOTAL MEDIA			
Network TV	1800	95	18.9
Print	2266	95	23.9
TOTAL	4066	95	42.8

Source: SMRB
        Telmar Group Inc.

MEDIA PLAN FOR BRK ELECTRONICS' AUTOSTAT

Client/Product: BRK Electronics
Agency: D'Arcy Masius Benton & Bowles

I. Media Objectives

To introduce and create awareness for Autostat

Target Audience

Reach an audience comprised of individuals who are:

- Strongly motivated towards convenience and/or comfort in the home
- Committed to adjusting their thermostats to save energy/money

Who, for media planning purposes, are defined as

- Adults age 25-54
- Income $25,000 plus
- Married with 3 to 4 people in household
- Own their own home

Special thanks to BRK Electronics and D'Arcy Masius Benton & Bowles.

The following table provides an analysis of the target definition.

Autostat
Media Target Audience Definition

	% U.S. Pop.	Heat/Energy %	Conservative** Index
Age			
25-54	54	65	121
Marital Status			
Married	62	78	123
Income			
$25,000+	42	54	127
Dwelling			
Own Home/Condo	72	88	122
Household Size			
3-4	39	45	115
AUTOSTAT TARGET*	11	18	167

 * Adults 25-54, Income $25,000 plus, Married with 3 to 4 people in household, homeowners.
** Purchasers of the following home improvements:
   • Automatic setback thermostat
   • Storm doors or windows
   • Weather-stripping
   • Insulation for ceiling, floor or wall

Data Source: Simmons Marketing Research Bureau

Geography

Concentrate advertising efforts within the largest U.S. cold weather markets where product has reached adequate distribution levels.

The following page lists the largest 25 markets with normal daily minimum temperatures of 40° or below during the winter season (November through January).

Distribution of these cold weather markets by Nielsen Marketing Regions is:

% U.S. TV Households by Nielsen Region

	Top 10 Markets	Top 25 Markets
Northeast	14.78%	18.16%
East Central	5.02	8.77
West Central	4.90	8.92
Pacific	1.35	2.96
	26.05%	38.81%

The number of advertised markets must be limited in order to allow for sufficient advertising impact within budget.

LARGEST U.S. COLD WEATHER MARKETS

MARKETS	% US TV HH	NORMAL DAILY MINIMUM TEMP. NOV	JAN
1. New York	7.71	40	25
2. Chicago	3.53	30	15
3. Philadelphia	2.96	36	24
4. Boston	2.30	39	23
5. Detroit	1.96	34	19
6. Washington D.C.	1.81	38	28
7. Cleveland	1.66	34	20
8. Pittsburgh	1.40	33	21
9. Minneapolis	1.37	24	3
10. Seattle	1.35	38	33
Sub-Total	26.05		
11. St. Louis	1.23	36	23
12. Denver	1.12	25	16
13. Baltimore	1.01	36	25
14. Hartford	.96	32	16
15. Portland, OR	.96	39	33
16. Indianapolis	.96	33	20
17. Kansas City	.85	33	18
18. Cincinnati	.83	34	22
19. Milwaukee	.82	29	11
20. Buffalo	.75	34	18
21. Columbus	.71	32	20
22. Grand Rapids	.68	34	19
23. Providence	.66	35	21
24. Salt Lake City	.65	28	19
25. Dayton	.57	32	20
Total:	38.81		

Source: U.S. National Oceanic and Atmospheric Administration 30 year study.

Timing

Begin advertising support mid-November to coincide with the onset of the cold weather/heating season.

Weight/Delivery

Build awareness rapidly, reaching a minimum of 80% of the target audience at an average of three times within the introductory advertising period.

Budget

To develop an advertising program within a media budget of $900,000 (gross).

In order to meet this objective and advertise at sufficient weight levels, the number of markets must be limited.

II. Media Strategies

The following strategies have been applied to a market list consisting of the top 10 cold weather markets. Media weight levels, costs, and audience delivery may change in the event that a different selection of markets is used.

Top 10 Cold Weather Markets

New York	Washington, D.C.
Chicago	Cleveland
Philadelphia	Pittsburgh
Boston	Minneapolis
Detroit	Seattle

Primary Medium

A base of spot television will be scheduled in the top 10 cold weather markets.

Rationale

- Provides immediacy and generates rapid awareness.
- Allows for target selectivity via specific daypart and program usage.
- Provides a visual showcase for introduction of new product.

Scheduling Tactics

- Weight: Approximately 115 Autostat Target Rating Points per week (translates to approximately 185 Household Rating Points/week).
- Flight: 3 weeks

- Scheduled Wednesday/Thursday/Friday only
- 30 second units
- Dayparts to be used:
  Prime
  — Most heavily-watched daypart—important for introduction
  — Builds audience reach for greater product awareness

  Late News/Late Fringe
  — Last-minute reminder before retiring
  — News environment

  Early Morning
  ("Today Show," "Good Morning America," "CBS Morning")
  — Reminder upon arising and a last-minute reminder before
    leaving home
  — News-type environment
- Distribution by daypart:

	% Distribution	Autostat Target Rating Points/Wk	Household Rating Points/Wk
Prime	10	12	18
Late News	45	52	76
Late Fringe	40	45	76
Early Morning	5	6	15
	100	115	185

See Appendix A for alternative daypart comparison.

Audience Delivery

The three-week schedule is estimated to deliver:

	Autostat Target	Households
Reach	81%	90%
Frequency	4.3	6.1

Secondary Media (National)

The Weather Channel, a national cable network, will be used to complement the spot television.

Rationale

- Provides focused editorial environment compatible with product.
- Offers opportunity for usage of customized dealer tags.
- Efficiently reaches 15.8 million subscriber households.
- 20% (3.1 million) are within top 10 cold weather markets.

Scheduling Tactics

- Flight: 3 weeks
- Scheduled Thursday/Friday only
- 5 announcements daily (= 30 announcements total)
- Early Morning/Late Evening
- Feature-program sponsorships:
  - "A Look Ahead/Weekend Outlook"
  - "Your Weather Channel Forecast/Low Temperature Map"
  - "Local Weather"
- 30 second units

National magazines will be used to complement the base of broadcast activity.

Rationale

- Highly targeted to potential purchasers of Autostat
- Supports sell-in of Autostat to the trade
- Extends national coverage against the target efficiently
- Allows for detailed copy

Magazine Selection Rationale

Magazines have been selected on the basis of:

- Target audience composition
- Editorial environment
- Cost efficiencies

See Appendix B, C, and D for circulation analysis, editorial profile and unit costs of magazines.

Selected Publications

- *House Beautiful*
- *Family Handyman*
- *Popular Science*

Description

- Monthly homeowner magazines
- December insertions will be scheduled in each magazine
- Page 4/C creative

Audience Delivery

The three insertions will deliver approximately:

	Autostat Target
Reach	11%
Frequency	1.8

III. Media Plan

BRK
Autostat Promotion

	November					December																
	M	T	W	TH	F	S	SU	M	T	W	TH	F	S	SU	M	T	W	TH	F	S	SU
	26	27	28	29	30	1	2	3	4	5	6	7	8	9	10	11	12	13	14	15	16

Spot Television
- 115 Autostat Target DRPs/Wk (185 HH GRPs/Wk)
- Prime/E. Morning/ L. News/L. Fringe
- :30s

Cable TV
The Weather Channel
- 5 Annc./Daily
- E. Morn./L. News
- :30s

Print
House Beautiful
Popular Science
Family Handyman

- Page 4/C

IV. Audience Delivery Summary
(Within Spot TV Markets)

	Reach	Frequency	Total DRPs*	Total HH GRPs
Spot Television	81%	4.3	345	555
The Weather Channel**	1%	3.0	3	5
Print	11%	1.8	20	N/A
Total	83%	4.4	368	

* Target Audience: Adults 25-54, Income $25,000 plus, married with 3 to
  4 people in household, homeowners
** Weather Channel audience delivery extrapolated from Mediamark Research
  Inc. study

V. Budget Summary

	Total Cost	
Spot Television	$818,000	92%
The Weather Channel	12,000	1%
Print	68,600	7%
Total Media Cost:	$898,600	

Appendix A
Alternative Daypart Comparison
(Based On Equal Costs Per Schedule)

Recommended Plan With Prime	Autostat Target Rating Points/wk	Household Rating Points/wk
Prime	12	18
Late News	52	76
Late Fringe	45	76
Early Morning	6	15
	115	185
3-Week Flight		
Reach	81%	90
Frequency	4.3	6.1
Approximate Total # Spots	68	

Recommended Plan With Prime	Autostat Target Rating Points/wk	Household Rating Points/wk
Without Prime		
Late News	55	81
Late Fringe	60	102
Early Morning	6	15
	121	198
3-Week Flight		
Reach	68%	78
Frequency	5.3	7.6
Approximate Total # Spots	79	

Appendix B
Magazine
Target Audience Composition
(Adults 18 + = 100 Index)

Female/Home Oriented	Autostat Index	Heat/Energy** Conservative Index
Better Homes & Gardens	140	126
Good Housekeeping	121	126
House Beautiful	165	149
Ladies Home Journal	122	121
McCall's	129	125
Do-It-Yourself Oriented		
Family Handyman	180	185
Mechanix Illustrated	157	158
Popular Mechanics	157	150
Popular Science	157	152
Additional		
Changing Times	180	114
Health	94	124

   * Selected Publications
  ** Purchasers of the following home improvements:
     • Automatic setback thermostat
     • Storm doors or windows
     • Weather-stripping
     • Insulation for ceiling, floor or wall

Data Source: Simmons Marketing Research Bureau

**Appendix C
Magazine
Circulation—Cost Detail**

Publication	National Circulation (000)	Effective Readership* (000)	Page 4/C Unit Cost ($)	Effective Cost Per Thousand ($)
House Beautiful	864	833	23,880	28.66
Family Handyman	1,250	657	18,990	28.90
Popular Science	1,838	794	25,730	32.40

* Effective Readership = Autostat Target Readership

**Appendix D
Magazine
Editorial Profile**

House Beautiful—a magazine designed for families interested in their homes and home furnishings. Architectural and decorating articles range from advance design concepts to practical home planning and maintenance information. The editorial content is primarily devoted to home furnishings, management and building; secondly, as a guide to good living, it regularly includes articles on travel, gardening, entertainment, food, liquor, music and beauty.

Family Handyman—is edited for the homeowner with an active interest in home improvement and home management. Major editorial categories include home remodeling, repair and maintenance, energy efficiency, home furnishings and decorating, yard and garden care. Additional themes include woodworking, auto maintenance, new products and general interest.

Popular Science—concentrates its editorial on new products that may be especially useful to people with strong interests in their homes, personal transportation needs and recreation. Major articles and departmental features cover such product areas as home workshop tools; automobiles, boats, and engines; garden and lawn equipment; electronic, TV, and photographic equipment; and recreational products.

Appendix E
Issue And Closing Deadline

	On Sale December Issue	Order Material Deadline
House Beautiful	November 20	September 25
Family Handyman	November 26	October 1
Popular Science	November 13	September 25

Appendix F
Spot Television
Market Costs

Markets	3 Weeks Total @ 115 DRPs/Wk*
New York	$182,139
Chicago	96,336
Philadelphia	94,980
Boston	126,111
Detroit	61,785
Washington D.C.	61,614
Cleveland	41,595
Pittsburgh	59,580
Minneapolis	51,249
Seattle	45,552
Sub-Total:	$820,941
St. Louis	$37,503
Denver	46,284
Baltimore	46,194
Hartford	50,427
Portland	33,093
Indianapolis	34,278
Kansas City	26,043
Cincinnati	27,348
Milwaukee	51,249
Buffalo	26,622
Columbus	28,422
Grand Rapids	19,545
Providence-New Bedford	22,485
Salt Lake City	23,382
Dayton	20,292

* Autostat target rating points. Translates to 185 Household rating points.

MEDIA PLAN FOR DUNLOP "DDH" GOLF BALLS

Client/Product: Dunlop "DDH" Golf Balls
Agency: J. Walter Thompson

I. Target Market

Frequent and Moderate Golfers defined primarily as men age 25-64 with household incomes of $20,000+ who play at least 12 rounds and/or days of golf per year

A. Frequency of play:

	SMRB*	+	A & S**	=	Consensus†
Frequent	20+ Days/yr		48+ Rounds/yr		
Moderate	5-19 Days/yr		12-47 Rounds/yr		Frequent/Moderate Golfers
Light	1-4 Days/yr		1-11 Rounds/yr		

B. Heavy user concept (A & S) strongly shows frequent and moderate golfers are key:

Rounds Played	% Rounds Played	% Total Players	Index (100 = Avg)
Frequent	61 } 94	23 } 62	265 } 152
Moderate	33	39	85
Light	6	38	16

Balls Used	% Balls Used	% Male Players	Index (100 = Avg)
Frequent	50 } 87	24 } 63	210 } 138
Moderate	37	39	94
Light	13	37	35

We are indebted to Alan H. Chaiet, Senior Vice-President, Media Director of J. Walter Thompson U.S.A./Atlanta, for providing this media plan.

C. Frequent/Moderate Golfer Demographics Indicate Men Age 25-64 with $20,000+ HH Income

	SMRB	**+**	**A & S**	**=**	**Consensus**
Sex					
% Male Players	74		77		
% Male Frequent Players	79		80	=	Male
% Male Moderate Players	77		77		

---

* Simmons Market Research Bureau
** Audits & Surveys, Inc.
† The "consensus" approach used here is based on combining the demographic and usage data from the two different research sources indicated.

SMRB	**+**	**A & S**		**=**		**Consensus**
		Index vs. Population (100 = Avg)				
Index vs. Population (100 = Avg) 20 + Days/yr		**By Rounds Played**	**Male Frequent**	**Male Moderate**		
Age						
45-54 = 138		25-34 120	105	155		25-64
		35-49 90	76	110 =		
55-64 = 174		50 + 141	169	91		

Index vs. Population (100 = Avg) 20 + Days/yr			**Index vs. Population (100 = Avg)**		
			Male Frequent	**Male Moderate**	
HH Income					
$20-$24M = 115		$15-$25M	108	125 =	$20M +
$25M + = 213		$25M +	143	132	
$35M + = 251					

II. Media Objectives

A. Environment

1. Utilize media that offer an environment highly compatible with target audience interests and creative objectives

a. Universe size perspective shows very limited but highly pinpointed audience potential

	SMRB	+	A & S		=	Consensus
	Millions (18+)	%US Pop. (18+)	Millions (12+) (18+)		% US Pop. (12+) (18+)	
Total Golfers	13.3	8.5%	15.8	14.5	8.9% 9.3%	*Only 8-9%U.S.*
Male Golfers	9.8	6.2%	12.2	11.2	6.8% 7.2%	*Only 6-7%U.S.*
Frequent Male Golfers	3.3	2.1%	2.9	2.7	1.6% 1.7%	
Moderate Male Golfers	3.5	2.3%	4.8	4.4	2.7% 2.8%	
Freq./Mod. TOTAL	6.8	4.4%	7.7	7.1	4.2% 4.5%	*Only 4-5%U.S.*

b. Target audience interests suggest that most mass media generate too much waste circulation and that environmentally targeted, highly concentrated vehicles are key.

B. Seasonality

1. Schedule advertising media weight to lead and slightly overlap the prime golf season.
   a. The golfball pro shop sales curve peaks April-August; however, the best national potential for the new ball is to lead the season early, then strongly build the national intro in March/April, and sustain through September when sales are still relatively strong.

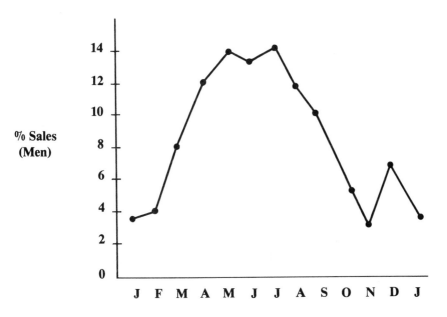

   b. Consider the bump in December for future Christmas season promotional opportunity.

C. Geography

1. Concentrate advertising on a national basis with additional emphasis in selected Sunbelt markets to capitalize on the extended golf season in theses areas.
   a. Pro golf ball shipments by region generally follow the start of the golf season, with Sunbelt areas beginning far before the rest of the country

Florida, S. Cal., Texas, Arizona, Hawaii	9/15 ⎫ 5-Month Separation
Mid South	2/15 ⎰
Midwest and North	3/15 ⎱ 6-Week Separation
Far North	4/1 ⎭

   b. Emphasize 14 major markets within the Sunbelt (14% of U.S.) in January and February when more Golf media become available, closing dates are realistic, and the 4th Quarter diversions of new car intros, national and local elections, and holiday advertising are over.

D. Impact

1. Develop target audience reach and frequency levels to generate top-of-mind awareness as follows:

	Intro (2 months)				Sustaining		Total Year			
	Sunbelt		National		Sunbelt & National		Sunbelt		National	
	Reach	Avg. Freq.	Reach	Avg. Freq.	Reach	Avg. Freq.	Reach	Avg. Freq.	Reach	Avg. Freq.
Period	85%	20.0	85%	14.0	85%	15.0	90%	35.0	90%	30.0
4-wk	80/6.0				70/4.5		Not Applicable			

   a. It is felt that near saturate unduplicated reach levels against the Frequent and Moderate Golfer target audience are necessary to introduce the new product, and that maximum affordable frequency is desirable to drive home the creative message on a continuous basis to maintain top-of-mind awareness during the golf season.
   b. Given the highly selective nature of the target audience, maximum reach levels within the limits of appropriate environmental media types will be achieved.

E. Flexibility

1. Maintain the flexibility necessary to accommodate opportunities or changes in marketing direction, as well as to make use of executional leverage and timing advantages.
   a. Budgets need to be as flexible as possible to be available for any shifts in strategy.
   b. Media buys should be made when the buyer knows the market is right for savings opportunities and can utilize the Agency's buying leverage.

III. Media Strategy

A. Suggested Media

1. National
   - Network Television Golf Tournaments
   - National Golf Enthusiast magazines

2. Sunbelt
   - Spot Television Golf Tournament (South California, Texas, Arizona, Florida, Hawaii)
   - Regional Editions of Golf Enthusiast Magazines

B. Rationale

1. TV Golf Tournaments
   a. Highly concentrated reach against the Frequent/Moderate Golfer target group.

      SMRB: 66% of target audience watch regularly
      1 commercial develops a 35 rating against the target audience
      26.8% of total audience is in target group
      Target audience concentration (index 989) is 3.4 times higher than next highest show
      A & S: 69% of Frequent Golfers watch regularly or at particular times
      48% of Moderate Golfers watch regularly or at particular times

   b. Environmentally and editorially matched to the target audience. Focus groups reported golfer "learned about new equipment on televised golf tournaments."

    c. Ability to communicate an intrusive introductory ad sustaining sales message via the unique elements of sight, sound and motion.

    d. Allows for multiple exposure impact each day of the weekend events, plus the added bonus of "sponsorship billboards" in network telecasts.

    e. Very efficient target audience delivery of $15-$20 CPM (5-10 times less than other Network Sports/Prime programs)

    f. Effectively satisfies creative requirements.

    g. Geographically flexible through use of Spot TV.

    h. Highly merchandisable to the sales force and pro shop trade. Focus group pros claimed "advertising does create a demand, especially TV advertising during tournaments."

2. Golf Enthusiast Magazines *(Golf* and *Golf Digest)*

    a. Increase reach in vehicles with heavy concentration of the target group.

> **SMRB:** *Golf* (circulation = 725,000) reaches 16.8% of the target group
>
> *Golf Digest* (circulation 1,000,000) reaches 23.1% of target group
>
> Combined target audience unduplicated reach is 30% with 1.3 frequency
>
> 31.0% of *Golf* total readers are in target group
>
> 37.6% of *Golf Digest* total readers are in target group
>
> Target group concentration (*Golf* index = 1,148, *Golf Digest* index = 1,393) is 2.5-3.0 times higher than the next highest magazine

    b. Environmentally and editorially matched to the target audience. Focus group golfers said they "learned about new equipment from advertising in golf magazines *(Golf Digest* and *Golf* mentioned most frequently)."

    c. Ability to convey a strong, visual message with the opportunity for long sales copy and high quality 4-color reproduction.

    d. Allows for use of high impact space units, especially during introductory months.

    e. Efficient target audience delivery of $20-$25 CPM is less than one-half of the CPM of publications like *Sports Illustrated,* for example.

    f. Effectively satisfies creative requirements.

    g. Geographically flexible via regional editions.

    h. Highly merchandisable to the sales force and pro shop trade who also read these publications and know that the target audience does.

IV. Media Tactics

A. TV Golf Tournament Tactics

1. Lead the season nationally with Network introduction in the Bob Hope Desert Classic (January) and the Bing Crosby Pro-Am (February), the 2 highest rated tournaments of the year. Advertising in these pre-season events will begin to create early inroads for the new ball idea/concept and have psychological overtones as the traditional harbingers of spring.
2. Heavy-up in the Sunbelt markets within the top 100 TV areas* in January and February with Spot TV in two additional tournaments per month.
3. Strengthen the national introduction in March and April with three network tournaments per month.
4. Sustain Network schedules with two tournaments per month through the prime season (including all "Grand Slam" events).
5. Each tournament will run two :30s per day Saturday and Sunday, or four :30s total for impact (plus "billboards" as earned).
6. Negotiate rates via budget flexibility and the agency's buying leverage.

*Spot TV markets:	Miami	Waco/Temple
	Tampa/St. Pete.	Los Angeles
	Orlando/Daytona	San Diego
	W. Palm Beach	Phoenix
	Austin	Tucson
	Houston	Honolulu
	San Antonio	El Paso

B. Golf Enthusiast Magazine Tactics

1. Introduce regionally in South and Western editions with 3-page, 4-color (4/c) Bleed units in January and February.
2. Introduce nationally with 3-page, 4-color (4/c) Bleed units in March and April.
3. Sustain schedules with 4-color (4/c) Bleed Pages monthly through September.
4. Negotiate desirable positions (center spreads, covers, gatefolds, far forward, right hand, opposite editorial).

DUNLOP "DDH" GOLF BALLS
Consumer Advertising
Media Schedule

	Jan	Feb	Mar	Apr	May	Jun	Jul	Aug	Sept	Total Cost (000)
TELEVISION GOLF										
Network Golf Tournaments* # Tourneys/# 30's	1/4	1/4	3/12	3/12	2/8	2/8	2/8	2/8		$1,338.1
Spot TV Golf Tournaments # Tourneys/# 30's	2/8	2/8								88.6
								TOTAL TV		$1,426.7
GOLF ENTHUSIAST MAGAZINES										
Golf										
Regional 3-page 4/c Bleed	■	■								$ 54.3
National 3-page 4/c Bleed			■	■						96.3
National Page 4/c Bleed					■	■	■	■	■	80.2
										230.8
Golf Digest										
Regional 3-page 4/c Bleed	■	■								$ 74.1
National 3-page 4/c Bleed			■	■						133.0
National Page 4/c Bleed					■	■	■	■	■	110.9
										318.0
							TOTAL MAGAZINES			$ 548.8
							TOTAL CONSUMER			$1,975.5

*Includes: Bob Hope, Bing Crosby, U.S. Open, British Open, PGA

REACH/FREQUENCY DELIVERY

		INTRO		SUSTAINING	TOTAL YEAR	
		Sunbelt	National	Sunbelt and National	Sunbelt	National
TV						
	Period	85%/19.8	85%/13.2	85%/13.2	85%/32.9	85%/26.4
	4-week	72%/5.8		65%/4.3	Not Applicable	
Magazines						
	Period	40%/3.9	35%/2.3	42%/2.7	46%/8.2	44%/6.3
	4-week	30%/1.3		30%/1.3	Not Applicable	
Total						
	Period	87%/21.1	86%/14.0	87%/15.2	88%/36.1	88%/28.7
	4-week	77%/5.9		72%/4.4	Not Applicable	

MEDIA PLAN FOR GENERAL FOODS' JELL-O BRAND GELATIN

Client/Product: General Foods' Jell-O Brand Gelatin
Agency: Young & Rubicam

SECTION I—MARKETING BACKGROUND

1. ADVERTISING PERIOD:

Fiscal Year 1984 (April 1983-March 1984)

2. MEDIA BUDGET: $20.0MM

3. MARKETING BACKGROUND

A. Competitive Frame

Jell-O Gelatin's primary competitive frame is the light dessert segment. It, however, must maintain a competitive awareness of the heavy dessert segment as well. The total gelatin market maintains a small (5%) share of the total sweet food market based on 1978 figures.

Within the Sugar Based Gelatin (SBG) market, Jell-O Gelatin (JOG) competes with Royal (20% share) and various private label and generic brands (10% share). JOG has maintained its share at the 70% level over the past 10-year period.

We are indebted to General Foods and Young & Rubicam for providing this media plan.

131

B. Competitive Advertising Expenditures

Sweet Food Category

In FY'82, Gelatin maintained a 16% share of Dessert Category spending with total expenditures of $12,447M. This compares with a 24% share in FY'81 when total spending was $16,966M. (See Exhibit A and B).

Light Dessert Segment

Within the Light Dessert segment (excludes cakes and pies), Gelatin held a 20% share of advertising expenditures in FY'82, ranking Gelatin behind the Pudding and Cookie Categories in total spending. In FY'81, Gelatin was the Light Dessert segment's spending leader with a 29% share of total expenditures.

Gelatin Category

JOG's substantial share of advertising expenditures within the Sweet Food Market is attributed to its aggressive spending position. While JOG spending decreased by 30% in FY'82 versus FY'81 to $10,707M, the Brand maintained a commanding 88% of all Gelatin advertising expenditures. This is down from a 92% share during FY'81.

C. Advertising Awareness

Although JOG enjoys universal Brand awareness, advertising awareness dropped considerably between FY'80 and FY'82

	FY'80	FY'81	FY'82
Brand Awareness	100%	100%	100%
Advertising Awareness	61%	62%	52%

Source: G.F.

D. FY'84 Outlook

Pricing/Spending Strategy

JOG will adopt a more aggressive spending philosophy in recognition of the Brands' "market responsibility" to support the sugar base gelatin market. The FY'84 AFP spending level is 50% greater than year-end FY'83.

The Brand will forego all pricing action in FY'84 until the MQ to improve JOG's price relationship with other sweet foods and private label/generics.

Advertising Strategy

For FY'84, advertising support will be directed behind more usage-oriented applications targeted against current JOG heavy users (3 + packages/month).

In the past, the brand has targeted its programs against the traditional family unit (husband works, wife and children at home). These households now represent 15% of total U.S. Over the past 20 years, the traditional family has given way to emerging target segments with different profiles (working women, singles, empty-nesters). These lifestyle shifts have had a profound effect on food behavior; in-home meals have declined, less time is available for food preparation, fewer formal meals are served and snacking behavior has increased.

Throughout this period of change, JOG maintained the traditional family as its target. As a result, media selection was consistently broad based, and lacked the pin-point targeting and saliency necessary to communicate relevantly with the new emerging user groups.

E. Geography

While JOG is nationally distributed, Brand Development tends to skew to the South, Central and Eastern Regions. Low Brand Development in the Western Region is a function of strong Royal penetration. The Southern and Eastern Regions show strength, though they amount to only 11.1% and 10.2% of volume, respectively.

	REGION				
	WEST	CSO	CENTRAL	SOUTH	EAST
BDI	78	91	110	149	130
% Volume	26.9%	20.3%	31.5%	11.%	10.2%

Source: Nielsen

F. Seasonality

JOG sales are relatively flat with a slight skew in usage to SQ and relative weakness in JQ. This is consistent and corresponds with consumption.

	VOLUME INDEX*	% CONSUMPTION
JQ	91	22
SQ	112	28
DQ	97	25
MQ	101	25

* Indexed to Average Quarter Volume

Source: G.F.

G. Purchase Cycle/Pack Rate

The total number of packages purchased within a year has decreased substantially since 1978. Research suggests that this is the result of a decline in the number of purchase occasions.

The Brand's current strategy focusing on developing greater frequency of use among heavy users should serve to moderate the decline in purchase occasions.

H. Serving Occasion

The decision to serve Gelatin takes place approximately nine hours before it is served while actual preparation takes place six hours prior to serving. Dessert usage represents the majority of Gelatin usage.

Consistent with traditional usage patterns, meal occasions account for the majority of Gelatin consumption.

I. Promotion

JOG has partnered with Cool Whip in a promotional effort designed to stimulate purchase. Twenty-eight million "cents off" pop-up coupons will be delivered via two-thirds page spread scheduled for July and August insertions in consumer magazines.

Additionally, the Brand will participate in The Recipe Booklet promotion which will incorporate all Brands within the Desserts Division. This promotion will be self-liquidating and is scheduled for MQ FY'84.

J. Key Marketing Objective/Strategy

The overall marketing objective for Jell-O Gelatin in FY'84 is to maintain volumes at current levels. This will be accomplished by holding the frequency of use among JOG's heavy user franchise via usage oriented programs.

EXHIBIT A
DESSERT CATEGORY ADVERTISING EXPENDITURES
FISCAL YEAR 1982

CATEGORY	MAGAZINES ($000)	NEWSPAPER/ SUPPLEMENTS ($000)	NETWORK TV ($000)	SPOT TV ($000)	NETWORK RADIO ($000)	OUTDOOR ($000)	TOTAL ($000)	SUB-CATEGORY %	TOTAL CATEGORY %
HEAVY DESSERT SEGMENT									
Cakes, Pies, Pastries	701	—	10,110	7,171	—	—	17,982	100	23
TOTAL HEAVY DESSERT SEGMENT	701	—	10,110	7,171	—	—	17,982	100	
%	4	—	56	40	—	—	100		
LIGHT DESSERT SEGMENT									
Cookies	924	1,046	8,854	2,360	414	9	13,607	22	17
Fruits	1,623	205	3,192	3,613	—	375	9,008	15	11
Yogurts	340	17	—	4,708	—	—	5,065	8	6
Ice Cream & Sherbert	269	—	—	4,565	—	40	4,874	8	6
Gelatin	4,353	—	6,349	1,745	—	—	12,447	20	16
Pudding	4,091	—	11,298	935	—	—	16,324	27	21
TOTAL LIGHT DESSERT SEGMENT	11,600	1,268	29,693	17,926	414	424	61,325	100	
%	19	2	48	29	1	1	100		
TOTAL DESSERT CATEGORY	12,301	1,268	39,803	25,097	414	424	79,307		100
%	16	2	50	32	*	*	100		

* Less than 1%

SOURCE: LNA '80-81

EXHIBIT B
GELATIN ADVERTISING EXPENDITURES
FISCAL YEAR 1982

Brand	Magazines $(000)	Newspaper/ Supplements $(000)	Network TV $(000)	Spot TV $(000)	Total $(000)	%
Jell-O Gelatin[1]	2,613.0	—	6,349.0	1,745.0	10,707.0	86
Knox Gelatin[2]	1,517.0	—	—	—	1,517.0	12
Royal Gelatin	222.6	—	—	—	222.2	2
Total	4,352.6	—	6,349.0	1,745.0	12,446.6	100

[1] Includes Partnerships: Birds Eye Cool Whip, Dream Topping, Pudding Desserts, Betty Crocker Cake Mixes.
[2] Includes Partnerships: Keebler's Ready Crust, COS Products, Sweet 'N Low Sugar Substitute, Blue Diamond Almonds.

SECTION II—STRATEGIC DECISION SUMMARY

1. PROSPECT AUDIENCE

A. Basic Designation

Homemakers who are heavy (3 + packages/month) users of Jell-O Gelatin.

B. Demographic

Advertising will be directed at current heavy users of JOG, defined as women over 50 years of age, who are not employed outside of the home.

C. Psychographic

She is a convenience-oriented woman who is experiencing a new independence and self-sufficiency. Although she used to enjoy frequently serving creative desserts to her entire family, she still takes pleasure in her husband appreciating her dessert preparations. She is active, with a renewed concern about health and foods.

Her family size is smaller now, and she is expecially concerned that food preparations offer a minimum of waste.

2. MEDIA STRATEGIES

A. Geography

Advertising will be primarily national since:

- the JOG franchise is well developed nationally and requires national support to maintain the franchise.
- geographic variations in volume are due primarily to fluctuations in frequency of use. Since FY'84 advertising is directed against heavy users, national advertising against these prospects should help to mitigate regional inconsistencies.
- national media provides the most cost efficient means of reaching JOG prospects.
- JOG is the SBG category leader, and has a market responsibility to support the category on a national basis.

Local advertising will be considered in support of high Brand Development regions should funding become available and after the national effective reach goals are attained.

B. Continuity

The Brand will advertise as continuously as possible, since:

- usage-oriented creative will focus on simple, everyday applications of JOG, arguing for continuity.
- analysis suggests that Brand volumes are maximized through maintenance levels of ongoing support rather than flighted periods of heavy activity.

C. Seasonality

Jell-O Gelatin will align advertising with quarterly usage patterns, and adjust television spending according to media efficiency idices.

	JQ	SQ	DQ	MQ
% Consumption	22	28	25	25
Efficiency Index*	106	91	111	92
Ideal % Funds	23	25	28	23
Ideal Spending	$4,600M	$5,200M	$5,600M	$4,600M
%GRPs	22%	28%	25%	25%

*Based on Early News and Day CPP

D. Communication Objectives

Communication goals have been established for the FY'84 campaign encompassing both primary and secondary media.

1. Effective Frequency

A minimum typical four-week effective frequency level of 3 + is recommended for JOG in FY'84. An analysis of a variety of marketing, media, and communication factors, and JOG's position relative to each of these factors, were used to set the effective frequency level (Exhibits I-III).

2. Effective Reach

Reach goal has been established at 75% of the target at the typical effective frequency level of 3 + . Since media selection will be based on vertical selectivity, this goal represents what can pragmatically be termed the maximum reach attainable at the specified effective frequency level.

E. Promotion

Every effort to enhance the synergy between advertising and promotional activity will be made. For example, during the JOG/CW promotion periods of SQ, media will be planned and scheduled to improve the overall communications of promotion. This will also be true with the Dessert Divisional Promotion scheduled for MQ.

F. Media Vehicle Selection

The FY'84 advertising strategy to promote simple usage and recipe ideas relies heavily on the combined ability of television and print executions to help create the necessary "consumer pull" to maintain usage behavior.

While television will help seat the usage idea, print media will emphasize the various product applications and recipe ideas, and tie them back under a Key Brand selling idea/umbrella theme.

Media vehicles will be chosen according to their ability to enhance communication with the specific target group consumers thereby lending saliency and relevancy to the Brand.

1. Television

Television will be the Brand's primary medium for FY'84 because it:
- can be selectively scheduled by daypart/programming to deliver the JOG heavy user base according to specific target group preferences.
- provides the audio/visual capability useful to effectively communicate an emotionally oriented "umbrella" campaign.
- has the qualities of sound and motion to communicate the unique attributes of JOG.
- can be utilized to demonstrate the convenience and ease of preparation of the JOG recipe ideas.

2. Daypart Selection

Dayparts will be selected according to their ability to deliver each target group within the daypart containing the highest concentration of target prospects:

Television Daypart	Women 50+
Early News	167
Day	152
Late Night	106
Prime	104
Early Morning	159

Source: SMRB 1981

a. *Early News* will be the Brand's primary daypart because:
  • News delivers the greatest concentration of users.
  • JOG can capitalize on strong viewer loyalties to generate program association and build frequency against older users.

b. *Day Network* will be JOG's secondary daypart since it:
  • provides excellent and efficient coverage of the target, who tends to be non-working.
  • offers time-of-day appropriateness to prepare JOG for dinner service.

c. *Early Morning Information* will be considered as a secondary daypart for targeting users since:
  • EMI has a high shew to the JOG heavy user.
  • EMI is environmentally similar to Early News.
  • it can offer time-of-day advantages relative to JOG preparation.

d. *Cable Television and Syndication* will be considered since specific networks and programs:
  • deliver a high concentration of target prospects.
  • contain programming emphasis on food preparation.

Due to the need to target with relative efficiency, and F'84 budget limitations, the Brand will not utilize Prime network or Late Night television.

3. Magazines

Magazines will be the Brand's secondary medium in FY'84. Magazines can:

  • provide vertical coverage of the target.

Maturity	341
Fraternal	231
Home Service	119
Woman Service	112

Source: SMRB 1981

  • provide special interest selectivity with editorial geared to the lifestyle/interests of the reader.
  • expand upon the usage idea communicated in television by providing excellent recipe dissemination potential.
  • significantly extend reach against the target group.
  • offer relevant editorial environments for food advertisements, to enhance communication effectiveness and heighten appetite appeal.

EXHIBIT I
JELL-O GELATIN
BRAND FREQUENCY FACTORS
FISCAL YEAR 1984

MARKETING FACTORS	JELL-O GELATIN'S POSITION RELATIVE TO MARKETING FACTORS	INDICATED FREQUENCY GOAL PER TYPICAL 4-WEEK PERIOD
Established vs. New Brand	Established Brand.	Low—2+
Household Penetration	Penetration is high among heavy-users households.	Low—2+
Brand Dominance	Dominant brand	Low—2+
Brand Loyalty	Loyalty has been strained due to price sensitivity of heavy users, resulting in some switching to private label and generic.	Medium—3+
Frequency of use	Heavy user frequency of use is high, but must be maintained in order to achieve F'84 Brand volume objectives.	High—4+
Brand Image	JOG enjoys a positive image among heavy users.	Low—2+
Competition	Little competition in the Sugar Based Gelatin sub-category, but JOG competes within the entire sweet foods category.	Medium—3+
Pricing	Lack of pricing in F'83 and F'84 has narrowed the historically high differential between JOG and other Sugar Based Gelatin and sweet food alternatives.	Low—2+

EXHIBIT II
JELL-O GELATIN
BRAND FREQUENCY FACTORS
FISCAL YEAR 1984

MARKETING FACTORS	JELL-O GELATIN'S POSITION RELATIVE TO MARKETING FACTORS	INDICATED FREQUENCY GOAL PER TYPICAL 4-WEEK PERIOD
New vs. Established Campaign	JOG will introduce a new usage-oriented campaign, ''Make it JELL-O and Create Sensation.''	Medium—3 +
Message Complexity	Relatively simple message.	Low—2 +
Message Uniqueness	JOG is the only national television advertiser in the Gelatin category.	Low—2 +
Message Variations (Pool Size)	JOG will have a moderate sized pool utilizing specific copy to the various target groupings.	Medium—3 +
Advertising Awareness	Awareness of JOG advertising (FUN) is high, but F'84 marks initial period of the new user-oriented campaign.	Medium—3 +

EXHIBIT III
JELL-O GELATIN
BRAND FREQUENCY FACTORS
FISCAL YEAR 1984

MARKETING FACTORS	JELL-O GELATIN'S POSITION RELATIVE TO MARKETING FACTORS	INDICATED FREQUENCY GOAL PER TYPICAL 4-WEEK PERIOD
Clutter Level	Day Network Television has high clutter levels, while News levels are lower.	Medium—3 +
Print	Print offers editorial adjacency opportunities which can significantly increase salience and relevancy of the advertising.	Low—2 +
Attention Levels	Attention levels in News are high.	Low—2 +
Continuity vs. Flighting	JOG will attempt to maximize continuity of support within the current spending parameters.	Medium—3 +
Selection of Media	Media selection will be based on target group interests and be pin-pointed with appropriate creative messages.	Low—2 +

SUMMARY

The result of analyzing all relevant marketing, communications and media factors indicates that a Medium 3 + frequency level is appropriate for JOG against each target groups for FY'84 on a typical 4-week period basis.

PLAN FOR GENERAL
ETTY CROCKER
NG

General Mills/Betty Crocker Frosting
m Harper Worldwide

in households of five or more people

	Year Around, with additional seasonal emphasis during Fall/Winter "Baking Season"
Regionality:	National media
Scheduling (R/F):	Establish representative reach/frequency levels vs. competitive brands
Generate broader reach/frequency in fall/winter quarters
Evaluate exposure at 3 + level
Maintain 2 weeks on/2 weeks off flighting pattern
Communications:	Capitalize on "Bake Someone Happy" equity
Budget Considerations:	Maintain 55%/45% first half/second half fiscal year spending split

*Details and rationale are developed by General Mills as part part of their confidential brand marketing plan.

Appreciation is extended to Michael White, Senior Vice-President and Director, Department of Media Resources of Needham Harper Worldwide, Inc., for permission to use this material.

III. Media Strategy

- To provide strong reach (90% +) against the target audience, at a 3 + frequency level, utilizing the following media:

  - Day/Prime Network TV: Primary Medium
  - Network Radio: Secondary Medium
  - Syndicated Radio: 52 Week Continuity
  - Magazines: Tactically

- This represents a partial shift in media strategy used in past years, adding radio to the previous mix of TV and magazines.

Rationale for Strategy Change

- Three factors necessitate the strategic shift to utilize a secondary medium in addition to network television.

  - Escalating TV costs
  - Increased competitive spending (TV)
  - Static Betty Crocker Frosting brand budget

- Use of radio as secondary, more efficient medium in conjunction with a television will give Betty Crocker Frosting media "Leverage"
- Continuation of an all TV strategy could cause further erosion of Betty Crocker Frosting's advertising "presence" vs. competing brands

Rationale for Use of Radio

Radio is being recommended as a secondary strategic media element in conjunction with Day/Prime Network TV since it:

- enables Betty Crocker Frosting to significantly extend reach and frequency beyond its television base throughout the year,
- represents use of a highly efficient medium to offset rising television costs,
- generates high levels of message frequency in registering the Betty Crocker name and "Bake Someone Happy" campaign equity,
- allows Betty Crocker Frosting to be in a medium not currently used by competition,
- builds upon the syndicated radio sponsorship launches in last fiscal year,
- The addition of Radio to Day/Prime Network Television allows Betty Crocker Frosting to:

- retain the use of television comparable to levels employed in the past during key periods while adding the highly efficient medium of radio,
- satisfy important strategic scheduling needs,
- have greater advertising "presence" vis-a-vis competitive brands.

IV. Media Tactics

Recommended Plan Summary

- Plan utilizes "Two On, Two Off" pulsing strategy (11 two-week flights) beginning in June and ending the following April.
- TV levels are constant throughout plan:

  - Day Network TV: 50 TRPs*/week (6 weeks)
  - Fall/Winter/Spring: 55 TRPs/week (16 weeks)

- Tactical print for new flavor of frosting used in November/December
- Plan spending summary:

By Medium		By Half Year	
TV	76%	1st Half	56%
Radio	19%	2nd Half	44%
Print	5%		
TOTAL	100%	TOTAL	100%

*Target Rating Points: Gross rating points as measured against the defined target audience only.

GENERAL MILLS, INC.
BETTY CROCKER FROSTING
MEDIA SCHEDULE

HH/W25-49 GRPS/WK	June	July	August	September	October	November	December
MAGAZINES/MONTH	30 6 13 20 27	4 11 18 25	1 8 15 22	29 5 12 19 26	3 10 17 24	31 7 14 21	28 5 12 19 26

Network Television :30

	June	July	August	September	October	November	December
Day	74/50	74/50	74/50	70/50	70/50	70/50	70/50
Prime				54/40	54/40	54/40	
TV R/F	42/2.4	42/2.4	42/2.4	67/2.7	67/2.7	67/2.7	42/2.4

Network Radio :30

	June	July	August	September	October	November	December
	65	65	65	45	45	45	45

Syndicated Radio :60

	June	July	August	September	October	November	December
	10/wk	10/wk	10/wk	10/wk	10/wk	10/wk	10/wk
Radio R/F	41/3.7	41/3.7	41/3.7	32/3.4	32/3.4	32/3.4	32/3.4
Total R/F	66/3.8	66/3.8	66/3.8	78/3.7	78/3.7	78/3.7	61/3.5

National Magazines P4Cs

	June	July	August	September	October	November	December
GRPs/# Insertions						88/5	88/5

MONTHLY TOTALS: $521.8 $456.5 $456.5 $1,161.4 $1,148.9 $1,398.9 $756.7
$ BY QUARTER: $1,434.8 $3,709.2
% BY QUARTER: 16%   40%
$ BY HALF YEAR: $5,144.0
% BY HALF YEAR: 56%

	January				February				March					April				May				$ (000)	% TOT
	2	9	16	23	30	6	13	20	27	5	12	19	26	2	9	16	23	30	7	14	21		
	67/50				67/50				67/50				67/50									$3,271.0	36%
	52/40				52/40				52/40													$3,633.3	40%
	67/2.7				67/2.7				67/2.7				42/2.4									$6,904.3	76%
	45				46				46				45									$1,152.4	12%
		10/wk				10/wk				10/wk					10/wk				10/wk			$650.0	7%
	32/3.4				32/3.4				32/3.4				32/3.4										
	78/3.7				78/3.7				78/3.7				61/3.5										
																					$500.0	5%

$934.2 $934.2 $1,123.1 $264.5 $50.0 $9,206.7   100%

$2,625.1 $1,437.6

28%   16%

$4,062.7

44%

GENERAL MILLS, INC.
BETTY CROCKER FROSTING
MEDIA RECOMMENDATION
WOMEN 25-49
DELIVERY SUMMARY

Period/Media Elements	Per Flight				Per Quarter			
	W25-49 TRPS	Gross Impressions (000)	# Occasions	Frequency/ Reach %	W25-49 TRPS	Gross Impressions (000)	# Occasions	Frequency/ Reach %
1st Quarter (June-August)								
Day Network	100	39,833	23	2.4/41.8	300	119,499	70	5.3/56.6
Network Radio	130	52,372	130	3.8/34.6	390	154,823	390	8.2/47.4
Syndicated Radio	20	7,967	20	2.5/ 8.0	130	51,624	130	8.0/16.2
Radio Sub-Total	150	60,427	150	3.7/41.0	520	208,151	520	9.2/56.8
TOTAL	250	100,260	173	3.8/65.7	820	327,650	590	10.1/81.3
2nd Quarter (September-November)								
Day Network	100	39,833	23	2.4/41.8	300	119,499	70	5.3/56.6
Prime Network	80	31,070	7	1.7/47.0	240	95,599	20	3.3/72.0
TV Sub-Total	180	70,903	30	2.7/66.8	540	215,098	90	6.4/84.8
Network Radio	90	35,491	90	3.3/27.0	270	107,549	270	7.5/36.0
Syndicated Radio	20	7,967	20	2.5/ 8.0	130	51,624	130	8.0/16.2
Radio Sub-Total	110	43,609	110	3.4/32.2	400	158,695	400	8.3/48.0
TOTAL	290	114,512	140	3.7/77.5	940	373.793	490	10.2/92.1

3rd Quarter (December-February)

Day Network	100	39,833	23	2.4/41.8	300	119,499	70	5.3/56.6
Prime Network	80	31,070	7	1.7/47.0	160	63,733	13	2.5/63.7
TV Sub-Total	180	70,903	30	2.7/66.8	460	183,232	83	5.7/81.3
Network Radio	90	35,491	90	3.3/27.0	270	107,549	270	7.5/36.0
Syndicated Radio	20	7,967	20	2.5/ 8.0	130	51,624	130	8.0/16.2
Radio Sub-Total	110	43,609	110	3.4/32.2	400	158,695	400	8.3/48.0
TOTAL	290	114,512	140	3.7/77.5	860	341,927	483	9.5/90.3

4th Quarter (March-May)

Day Network	100	39,833	23	2.4/41.8	200	79,666	47	3.8/52.0
Prime Network	—	—	—	—	80	31,866	7	1.7/47.0
TV Sub-Total	100	39,833	23	2.4/41.8	280	111,532	54	3.9/72.0
Network Radio	90	35,491	90	3.3/27.0	180	71,779	180	5.3/34.0
Syndicated Radio	20	7,967	20	2.5/ 8.0	130	51,624	130	8.0/16.2
Radio Sub-Total	110	43,609	110	3.4/32.2	310	123,681	310	6.9/45.0
TOTAL	210	83,570	133	3.5/60.5	590	235,213	364	7.0/84.6

Cume Year (June-May)

Day Network	1100	438,163	256	17.1/64.5
Prime Network	480	191,198	40	5.8/82.9
TV Sub-Total	1580	629,361	296	17.4/90.6
Network Radio	1110	442,545	1110	20.2/55.0
Syndicated Radio	520	207,132	520	26.0/20.0
Radio Sub-Total	1630	648,760	1630	26.7/61.0
TOTAL	3210	1,278,121	1926	33.3/96.4

ASSUMPTION: (Print ($500M) was excluded from this Analysis.

COMPETITIVE OVERVIEW*
BROADCAST DELIVERY SUMMARY

Company/Brand	1st Quarter June–August			2nd Quarter September–November			3rd Quarter December–February			4th Quarter March–May		
	W25-49 TRPS	Gross Impressions (000)	Frequency/ Reach (%)	W25-49 TRPS	Gross Impressions (000)	Frequency/ Reach (%)	W25-49 TRPS	Gross Impressions (000)	Frequency/ Reach (%)	W25-49 TRPS	Gross Impressions (000)	Frequency/ Reach (%)
GMI/Betty Crocker												
Recommended Media Plan (TV Only)												
Average												
Flight/Month	100	39,833	2.4/41.8	180	70,903	2.7/66.8	180	70,903	2.7/66.8	100	39,833	2.4/41.8
Quarter	300	119,499	5.3/56.6	540	215,098	6.4/84.8	460	183,232	5.7/81.3	280	111,532	3.9/72.0
Recommended Media Plan (TV & Radio)												
Average												
Flight/Month	250	100,260	3.8/65.7	290	114,512	3.7/77.5	290	114,512	3.7/77.5	210	83,570	3.5/60.5
Quarter	820	327,650	10.1/81.3	940	373,793	10.2/92.1	860	341,927	9.5/90.3	590	235,213	7.0/84.6
P&C/Duncan Hines												
Average												
Flight/Month	212	84,446	3.8/71.8	144	57,360	2.3/62.9	144	57,360	2.3/62.9	144	57,360	2.3/62.9
Quarter	689	274,449	10.1/81.3	468	186,418	5.5/84.5	468	186,418	5.5/84.5	468	186,418	5.5/84.5
Pillsbury/Pillsbury Plus												
Average												
Flight/Month	150	59,750	3.1/48.1	258	102,770	3.5/73.6	258	102,770	3.5/73.6	150	59,750	3.1/48.1
Quarter	300	119,499	5.3/56.6	688	274,051	7.9/86.7	860	342,564	9.7/88.5	300	119,499	5.3/56.6

* Based on Betty Crocker Media recommendation and projected competitive media plans.

Plan Flexibility Considerations

It is essential that integrity of the Media Plan be maintained. Below is a prioritization of the Media Elements. This prioritization is designed to determine how to cut media funds (if necessary) from the plan and maintain a strong presence in key periods.

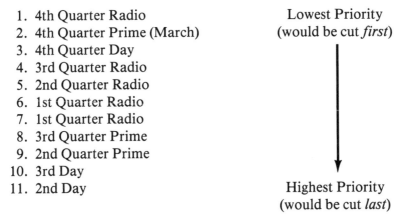

1. 4th Quarter Radio   Lowest Priority
2. 4th Quarter Prime (March)   (would be cut *first*)
3. 4th Quarter Day
4. 3rd Quarter Radio
5. 2nd Quarter Radio
6. 1st Quarter Radio
7. 1st Quarter Radio
8. 3rd Quarter Prime
9. 2nd Quarter Prime
10. 3rd Day
11. 2nd Day   Highest Priority
                                                      (would be cut *last*)

Rationale for Prioritization

- 4th Quarter elements most expendable because of least impact on annual volume
- Network Radio more expendable than television because of syndicated radio presence
- 1st Quarter Radio more important than 2nd or 3rd Quarter Radio because there is no Prime Time TV in the 1st Quarter Schedule
- 1st Quarter Day more expendable than 2nd and 3rd quarter television because impact is needed in key periods
- Day Network in 2nd and 3rd Quarters is last to be cut because presence in both key periods is more desirable than Prime impact in only one

Index

Other books on media from NTC Business Books

Advertising Media Planning (Second Edition) by Jack Z. Sissors and Jim Surmanek

Media Planning Workbook: with Discussions and Problems (Second Edition, Revised) by Jack Z. Sissors and William B. Goodrich

Media Planning: A Practical Guide by Jim Surmanek

Media Math: Basic Techniques of Media Evaluation by Robert W. Hall

Cable Advertiser's Handbook (Second Edition) by Ronald B. Kaatz

Effective Frequency: The Relationship Between Frequency and Advertising Effectiveness by Michael J. Naples